NEW CONTEXTS: 2

Ⓑ

First published in paperback and ebook
format by **Coverstory** *books*, 2021

ISBN 9781838232153 (paperback)
ISBN 9781838232160 (ebook)

www.coverstorybooks.com

Foreword

In many ways selecting pieces to be included in *New Contexts: 2* was a much more difficult task than it had been for the inaugural edition of *New Contexts: 1* published at the beginning of the year. This was primarily due to three factors.

The first was the breadth of the submissions. For *New Contexts: 2* the geographical spread of contributors is much greater with many more offerings from the United States and others from as far afield as Australia and New Zealand. Inevitably with such diversity of source comes a wider range of voices and styles - which is surely a good thing! - but this inevitably leads to some interesting dilemmas when trying to compare 'apples with pears'.

Secondly, the themes of the work offered for consideration were more varied, including - thankfully! - far fewer pieces that were Covid-related. There were an increased number of submissions which touched on fundamental topics such as sexuality, diversity, and the political (with a small 'p').

And thirdly, there were a greater proportion of prose submissions than for *New Contexts: 1* - and a small number of pieces that seemed to have their feet rooted in both poetry and prose camps.

All of which made the final selection challenging. There are pieces included here that probably would not have made it into *New Contexts: 1* - and vice versa.

Overall, I would like to believe that we have been able to strike an acceptable balance - prose versus poetry, the innovative versus the traditional - in terms of content, theme, and voice.

I hope you enjoy the collection.

Ian Gouge, September 2021.

Pears for Supper

I prepared pears today,
nothing fancy, no wine,
no sugar, no cream,
just fruit cored and peeled,
such a smooth baby's
bottom shape, so soft.

Pears give up their skins
so easily, a sharp knife,
three precise movements,
green farls binned and
the sweet white flesh slips
into bowls, fridge-ready.

They made a scratch lunch
with a glass of rose and
lumps of Cheddar, that last
time sitting in my sun-room,
idly listening to Audible, but
thinking all the while of loss —

the loss of my garden, its
steep slope, my blue & yellow
bedroom, my sunny lounge.
If only I could give it all up
as readily as pears their skins
I think, as I close the front door

and turn my key for the last time.

Moira Andrew

When Buzzards Descend

I
Go.
Read the scrolls of sky —

when buzzards dive
clouds turn sullen

no birds sing

the cathedral library of the sun
shuts down

shelves of the vault's best works
       empty out or drop to shadow —
             all birds, all leaves of literature
                 take flight.

II
                 When buzzard gods descend
         finches flee
     wrens dart to hedgerows
robins unstitch their songs —

         fall silent, perch still
    in archways.

III
I have seen other views
      heard other news
from buzzard tongues cried out
      from gaping beaks
           above Exmoor, where they float
      between beech crowns
over the winding Exe or River Barle

      or where they rise on spiral airways
         over ridges gashed
    with gorse and trefoil
        with hawkbit and blue scabious.

IV
This beauty — breathless —
all this they hold
in their keen ear, their sight
their cry of warning:

flutter of small wing, patter
of vole feet, shrew feet, mouse feet
on and under grass and wheat

as they wheel the roof
of the sun's high range
before they descend

dive for the wild joy of it
the jest of it
the sparring joust and play
the display of it — just that.

V
And when they seek a mate:
fling
flare
fold
flash
their gold-foil feathers
barred and striped in plural

then lift —
singular once again
to cry again

to hunt alone
above the open pages of the moors
above the fields and valley floors.

Lizzie Ballagher

Late Winter Poem

What are the words
for the things that aren't

those wisps of potential
inelegance fluttered away

remaining the leaden
unwished for tomorrows

their choices... unoffered.
I scarcely remember the time

daydreams weren't impossible —
when the world had our backs.

Always one step in front of the other
a word an afterthought ahead

and the inside
did not exist. That

was me in the mirror
and it was okay.

What to do now?
The essence is essentially

absent
from the core.

Clare Bercot Zwerling

Lost Correspondence

it needed to be written

I thought I would write you a letter
but later that thinking   grew latent
    it's sentiments unsent   the
sending seemed unsentimentally
self-seditious in light of the
unstated darkness undeniably
long laid below all our
surfaces yet above under
standing   you see it's all
still opening to me in the closing
of ears to the years' old
explanations   audible in their
falseness of truth and of trust

still I struggle

my brother

no pen clutched tightly by my fingers
loosening thoughts repressed
depressed and etched on any paper
handed to postman   to mailbox   to
rest in your hands
to crumple in waste can
a wasted effort reaching far
across your border   self imposed
    yourself imposed on this person
I'll never know again.

Clare Bercot Zwerling

The Lacquer Photo Album

I couldn't understand why my mother hated
it so much. To me – a child in dreary post-war
Britain – it was the loveliest thing I'd ever seen.

It was his most precious possession –
sole survivor from his army life, bought
from a craftsman in a Hong Kong market.

When occasionally it appeared from hiding,
I slid my hand across its hardened shine, traced
the inlaid pattern of mother-of-pearl and shells.

That old thing, she'd say, *it's falling apart!*
And was it any wonder – packed at the bottom
of his kitbag, shipped from conflict to conflict,

then heaped with others in a troop ship,
carrying him back to Blighty, to train,
for the Landings that ended his career.

Was she jealous of his time before they met –
girls posing in cheongsam; sari-clad women
on tea plantations, smiling at the camera?

Or was it seeing him in those distant places,
strong limbs tanned in khaki shorts,
knowing what happened next, what they'd lost?

Margaret Beston

The Last Time I Saw You

was when we bumped into each other
just by chance at the Bowes Museum,
both admiring the Silver Swan,
both of us far from home.

We listened as the curator
described in detail how 30 lbs
of silver were used to create
this splendid automaton
how it appeared at the Paris Exhibition,
was bought by Mr Bowes for a tidy fortune.

Before he turns the key to set
the life-like bird in motion, he lists
the 113 rings that allow its neck to bend
and arch as though preening, how twisted
glass rods give appearance of water,
how the 100 silver leaves decorating
edges of the pond were crafted
by a Parisian jeweller.

I think of you today, the happenstance
of us meeting all those years ago,
and I think of the Silver Swan,
its three clockwork hearts still working.

Margaret Beston

For Once, Goodbye

The last day he drips from my mouth the last day I am squished and made to feel unbeautiful I lay on the grass and feel things under me. Worms and ladybugs and deep marvellous roots that entangle me and release me from 19 months of being taken, fucked.

His lips taste like whiskey and I can't look at him the same way I did. Things used to have more magic. Now I am like the dirt on which I lie. Wash me away like mud and I will circle the drain slow and sexy.

He kisses me on the forehead and leaves me and I do not tell him that it is the last time. I have never had the strength for him, I have never had the strength to stand. I can tell it annoyed him.

"Take it," he would mutter and I could not take it. I will go to sleep with the fallen leaves and he will drive home and it will be the last night I feel the deep ache in my hips and spine.

Riley Burke

Pull Me

Pull from me peonies
and impatiens that breathe,
hot pink petals that expand and contract
and turn gray and saggy from too much cigarette smoke.

Pull from me a never-ending handkerchief
of 100 different colors
tied together end to end
so the little kids shriek in awe at the birthday party.

Pull from me the stick
the ooze
the 10 year old crying over the toilet,
"why is there blood?"

Pull my heart out
feel it in your fist.
Is it soft?
Warm, like how I felt when you first pushed into me

and sighed,
you feel good.

Pull my finger.
Fine, roll your eyes.
You remind me of my father
only younger.

Pull from me every tissue
and cell and atom
until I am a ghost
and you take me out dancing,
nice and empty, ready for you.

Riley Burke

Castles, Books, and Submarines

SOMEWHERE ON THE SOUTH SIDE OF CHICAGO:
May 12th, 1925. Dorothy "Dotsy" Elich was born under the sign of the bull and year of the Ox on the Chinese calendar. If that astrological mumbo-jumbo counts for anything, I attribute it to making my aunt the most stubborn and fiercest woman I know.

SWEET, STICKY DISNEYLAND:
"When I turned 20 I told myself I needed to get out of the house.
So instead of my sister,
who was too fragile to step out the door without a man to guide her,
I sucked it up and packed my bags. No risk no reward.
And as soon as I left the tirade of my parents,
I went to the only logical place I could think of.
Hot sun, smiling faces, cute caricatures running around...
They called it the happiest place on Earth for a reason, right?"

She moved into a dilapidated studio apartment about five blocks away from Disneyland California and commuted to work on foot. With the park in the middle of a staff expansion, corporate slapped Dotsy with the title of "management team member" without even reviewing her resume first (not that there would've been much on it, anyhow). Initially, she thought landing a job at the largest tourist trap in America was just the Disney magic rubbing off on her - after all, what a fantastic opportunity this was!

But Dotsy, to her dismay, would be horribly wrong.

From Mickey ears to castle T-shirts, she took inventory of the merchandise flooding the warehouses every day, then dished out paraphernalia until her arms wore out. This process, with marginal alterations, was repeated day after day for a year and a half. Dotsy always scorned her friends for being stuck in a hamster wheel of maternal monotony - cooking and cleaning and kissing their kiddos goodnight - but now she was stuck in the same hellish loop.

Every Monday through Friday, Dotsy plodded through the unforgiving sun watching children prance around with scuffed-up shoes and dried ice cream plastered on their faces like sticky birthmarks. She began to pity herself and every other depressed adult maintaining a happy-go-lucky facade for kids who barely noticed their existence.

"I realized that I needed to get out and make a difference in the world.
I felt stagnant after a while,
slipping further and further into a job and farther away from a career.
Disneyland taught me that those words have different meanings -

job and career -
and God help the poor souls who think they're the same."

THE ONLY MIRROR SHE OWNED:

Dotsy joined the Marines after the 1948 law that permitted women in the military. Even though she no longer feels comfortable delving into detail about her four-year term, she assures me it was good for her in the end. She remembers how it felt slipping on her uniform for the first time, the crisp, unforgiving fabric hiding her feminine curves to give off the illusion of a straight-cut figure. It made Dotsy feel like those plastic toy soldiers her older brother played with when they were kids: stout, stoic, and able to withstand a nasty tumble down the basement stairs.

"Too many times, being a woman stopped me from doing what I wanted.
I stood in my bathroom gawking at myself like I was Narcissus,
and in fact, I would've put him to shame.
That uniform was my escape -
a way to be powerful and serve a purpose."

Her gift from the U.S. government was stiffer than rigor mortis and valiant in its effort to make every movement laborious, but Dotsy didn't care. While every other doll-eyed woman was blissfully frying ham and eggs for her breadwinning husband and gaggle of cherry-lipped children, she was preparing for something bigger.

"I'd rather go to Hell and back than become a housewife.
Every poor woman trapped in that fantasy
was starring in their very own Groundhog Day.
I had friends whose schedules I memorized
because they did the exact same things at the exact same time
every single day of the week.
Not saying what they were doing wasn't important -
raising the next generation is a noble task, indeed -
but I wanted something more for myself:
a life of my own."

A DUSTY LIBRARY THAT HELD MORE THAN A DREAM:

According to Dotsy, being a lesbian in the 1950's was almost as dangerous as the Marines; the widespread homophobia in an era where many women existed as trinkets collecting dust on shelves was a dastardly combination for someone who planned on being neither of those things.

"It was like owning a speakeasy,
except the secret room downstairs was your heart
you only let people with the password into.
That's why I moved to California - to open my own speakeasy
and stop pretending I ran a run-of-the-mill business
without any hidden doors.

I couldn't get away with being gay at home.
My parents were smart and more judgemental than that lady on CBS.
…You like how poetic that was?"

The lady my aunt was referring to, as I later found out, was Judge Judy.

"I had been unsure of my sexuality for a while -
I always caught myself drooling over Audrey Hepburn instead of the Ken Dolls
co-starring in her films -
But the day I met Maggi Kennedy in the library was the day I knew
women were the only ones allowed in my speakeasy."

I acknowledge the Hollywood-levels of cliche surrounding the premise of meeting your lover in a library, but Dotsy's life was tremendously more interesting than half the movies these days. I suppose in this manner, it's only fitting.

She doesn't remember the name of the library, but she does recall the hexagon path leading up to the entrance and how hard she tried to avoid the tip of her kitten-heels falling into the cracks between the bricks. She remembers the way the dust particles, stirred up by the *whoosh* of the double doors swinging open, would float around the room like dandelion fuzzies. And most importantly, she remembers the glum face of the front desk clerk that was squashed under dainty hands and a name tag that simply read "Mag."

"Maggi looked bored to tears the first time I went in there.
And if I'm being honest, which you know I always am,
she looked just as bored each time after that. Except when I came in.
She had this sort of adorable pout -
almost as if there was a vendetta between herself and the wall clock across from her.
She would angrily stare it it down to intimidate the hands
into ticking faster than they should
so her gruelling shift would end.
It never worked, of course,
but that didn't stop the girl from trying."

Their first conversation occurred when Dotsy checked out two books about Belize and international tourism. After Maggi inquired if Dotsy planned on traveling while ringing her up, the small talk that followed quickly evolved into a lengthy conversation about foreign culture. Maggi, who had never been out of the country before, wrote short fantasy novels in her free time about the exoticies of overseas adventures. Dotsy, enamored by this, promised to indulge her with the details of her trip and perhaps photos upon returning. Catching Maggi up on the highlights of her which was something that became a regular occurrence.

Infatuated by Maggi's radiant smile and intellectual edge, simply pining after her from afar was something Dotsy no longer had the patience for. On a hazy day in September and donned in her Sunday best,

Dotsy strutted down that gilded brick pathway with fervor and finally asked Maggi out for coffee.

EGGSHELL LEATHER SEATS:

"The kiss happened after a drive-in movie.
I was so nervous I can't remember what was playing to this day.
Neither of us had revealed ourselves at that point -
we were both riding on the bold assumption that the other was gay.
Thank God we were right
because after I drove her home in my father's old Ford
I stole a quick kiss on the cheek when it was safe in the dark,
and then she stole one back on the lips,
and damn me if I was gonna let her have the last one
so I kissed her back a second time."

FRANCE, 1991:

Maggi and Dotsy traveled. And traveled. And went home to make sure their apartment hadn't burned down in their absence and then traveled some more.

They saw almost every region in the world in less than twenty years; no foreign language or culture was too daunting as long as the two of them faced the unknown together. My aunt - and I don't mean this as a hyperbole - is probably one of the most worldly and astute people in America. I remember hearing horror stories about some of her misadventures when I was younger, like when she traveled to China during the 1960's and lived off processed cheese balls for three days because the first restaurant she visited served her fried pigeon, or when she lost Maggi in France and only knew how to say *revoir!* and *oui oui!*

Maggi, whose parents emigrated from Paris, spoke the language fluently and was deigned to be more of a translator than a partner to Dotsy while they were in Marseille. She ordered all of Dotsy's meals (sometimes "inadvertently" asking for the wrong one if she was feeling particularly thorny) and constantly explained dialogue between the characters on the sitcoms that played on their hotel room TV.

"Maggi up and left in the middle of an evening stroll.
I remember bending down to fetch my runaway wallet
which had landed on the cobblestone street,
and when I stood back up to make a joke about my clumsiness
Maggi was nowhere in sight.
I wandered the square for the longest twenty minutes of my life before
I finally found the bastard picking flowers from a private garden closed off for the night.
I wanted so badly to be mad at her
but all I could do was stand there and laugh.
Moments like those are so small but the ones I look back on most fondly."

SHERMAN OAKS, CALIFORNIA:

And now, after a whirlwind of 96 years, Dotsy resides in a small yet chic bungalow on the quaint side of Sherman Oaks, California. Her traveling is mostly limited to grocery store trips and coffee shop runs, but her frail bones and sagging skin (which, she notes, is a sign that the devil is trying to drag her down to hell) hasn't taken the zeal out of her spirit. In fact, her mind is still acute enough to point out the sentence fragments and dangling participles in the writing that I send her; she's probably going to have a field day marking up this workshop when she reads it.

Dotsy attributes her shrewdness to constantly reading, whether it be skimming an academic essay or or browsing the daily newspaper. It's a hobby she initially loathed but begrudgingly came to love since the written word was Maggi's lifeblood as a writer. After her passing in 2017, my aunt has made exercising her brain her top priority in order to preserve the encyclopaedia of memories they've made together.

"Maggi's been gone for four years and I miss her more than ever.
But I've got her here with me every time I wake up
and every time I go to sleep.
Her book collection still takes up half the shelves in the house
and her stories are kept in the desk
I do all my brooding on."

She paused to flip a page of something. Possibly a photo album.

"People nowadays seem to be obsessed with minimalism and throwing away
everything they own until they've got nothing left.
But I say a big fuck you to that. Pardon my François.
Because when you're dead and gone, your imprint on the world goes with it.
Memories are only good when you've got a working brain to keep them in.
Maggi survives in my head for now,
But when I'm dead she will still be alive through the things she owned
and the things she touched and the things she loved.
and I think someone like her, and hell, maybe even someone like me,
deserve to keep on living."

Sarah Butkovic

22

Privilege

I can't complain. I'm privileged. I can't be upset. I've got it good. And growing up... it must have been easy. It must have been great. A real cakewalk. A breeze. My folks, they had money. And no one hit me. No-one hurt me. No. Not like *that*. Those antidepressants I didn't want that I had to swallow. You know, the ones that made me feel dead. The ones that meant I couldn't get hard. The ones that made me think about suicide for the first time in my life, because, you know, I'm told I'm 'depressed.' 'I'm in danger.' Those pills that 'I need' proved to me that I wasn't actually happy. I guess I just thought that I was. But that couldn't be. Why else all the prescriptions my mother seemed to collect for me like so many fine trophies? When it came to medication she devoutly adhered to 'the more the merrier.' Yeah, the cocktails of drugs... those were fine. After all, I've got it good.

Sure, my older sister did things to me. She pulled down my pants and underwear. She showed me things that blew my mind. She made me not want to eat for days. But that's nothing. I mean, some kids are hungry. Can you believe that? Don't you worry about the little things. Stop complaining. Just don't tell anyone. Okay?

I had a lot of Christmas presents to open, it's true. But I also had a lot of things I believed were worth saying. I actually thought I had some great things to share, to express. But I was told those things were a one way ticket to being a nobody. A loser. 'Don't do *that*' I was told. 'You'll end up a bum.' You know, things like drawing, painting, pretending... things that will make you a bum. And why would I do those things? I had access to the golf course.

I remember being rebuked for jerking off. I was eleven or twelve or somewhere around there. Around the same time my older sister first put me in her mouth. Showed her friends. That was a couple of years before the antidepressants. The ones that opened me up to the notion of death. Of achieving an end. Like pressing the 'off" button to the video game console I was so lucky to have. The option to end it all.

When I discovered I could do to myself what my sister had done to me it was a bit of a revelation. I learned the word. 'Masturbation.' It sounded scientific to me at the time. It sounded sophisticated. I kind of overdid it. I'd do it at night before I fell asleep. My bed sheets... they'd seen better days.

My mom - after I said to my older brother his underwear will have skid marks because he farted like a trumpet being played underwater - she says to me, 'You're one to talk, I've seen the state of your bed sheets.'

'What?' My brother asked. 'Has James been shitting in the bed?'

'No!' I shouted. Looked at my mom and begged her with a look to leave it at that. She did. Bless her. But she also whispered in my ear that I was a bad, bad boy and that I was on the path to become a dropout. A loser. A nobody.

'Be like your sister,' she'd say. The sex offender.

'Be like your brother,' she'd tell me. The bully. The straight shooter. The guy that loved sports and hated fags.

'Stop those damned doodles and scribbling and study, for God's sake!' My mom said like those little maps I drew were the plague.

My sister was across the table and looked at me like she owned me. My brother shovelled eggs down his throat, he was oblivious, uncaring.

'If you don't get a degree you'll be an addict. You'll be loser. You'll have no future. You may as well be dead. You'll be dead, in any case, to me.'

Just give me a handful of those fancy antidepressants. That will do the trick and save you from the university bills.

I'm privileged. I've got it great. My sister is married and that is good because she no longer makes me feel like I'm hers to play with. My brother is playing football down south in Florida, which is fantastic because I'm no longer bruised and battered. My dad, he's at work, like he always is, or out of town, like he often is, so I don't need to see him that much which is what I am used to, and that's okay.

My mom. My mom... she still texts me all the time. She still calls and emails. She reminds me that I need to grow up. Do better. Raise a family and make something of myself.

I told her about my fiancé. She jumped for joy. I told her my fiancé's name. Tom. She went limp. Dead. It was like she was the one taking those antidepressants she made me swallow when I didn't even know what depression was. When I was happy so long as I could 'doodle' or 'scribble.'

James and Tom. Disgraceful. Obscene. *Perverse*.

I wasn't a bum. I had escaped that fate, despite my choices that all but guaranteed that outcome. I wasn't an addict either. I dodged that bullet. Because everyone knows, you are either hugely successful or homeless and on drugs. Those are your options. Make your *choice*.

Somehow I was neither. An anomaly. I wasn't on drugs and I didn't live under a bridge. I wasn't anyone's boss and I hadn't climbed a single rung on the financial ladder. I was working retail and I was sober. I made more than minimum wage. So there was that.

No. I wasn't a bum. I wasn't an addict. But I wasn't what my parents thought I would be. I wasn't even sure I knew what I was. I mean, I love Tom. I do. But we aren't conventional. Even being queer, we aren't the standard mold. We don't have sex. My sister turned me off from all of *that*. I just knew I was happy - sort of - because Tom loves my doodles, loves my scribbles. I was content - kind of - because I wasn't told what an awful person I would become or what heinous fate I might endure if I did or didn't do this or that. I wasn't urged to play my cards right and hide who I was so long as I played the game with its rigid rules. Walk the narrow path.

Deviate, and be damned.

But I'm privileged. I've got it good. Just look at my sister, mother of three. Married to a lawyer. Just look at my brother, an architect with a roof over his head of his own design. Good people. Good stock.

Me, I'm privileged. I don't have the right to complain. And why would I? I'm not a bum. I'm not an addict. No-one told me when growing up there were so many other ways to be unhappy. To feel like I did when I was taking 100 milligrams of Zoloft. But here I am. Still privileged. Still sad to be alive.

I guess it could be worse. I could be a bum and be happy. I could be an addict and have a drive, be inspired. I could be my sister, mother of three. My brother, the guy with a career. I think I'll just close my eyes. I'll pretend. I'll doodle a little life for myself. I'll scribble a golden future.

I'm privileged. No excuses.

I've got it good. No complaints.

James Callan

In the Photo, My Mother Wears Her Red Cross Uniform

It's sometime in the early 1940's—
her back straight, her hair an impossibly
smooth pageboy. She looks like Ingrid Bergman.
Beautiful. Untouchable. In charge.
I am not in the picture but that is the image
I carry of a woman, of how women are.
Busy. Pristine. Coming to the rescue.

After my stepfather drove off, Mother
promised there would be no more men in her life,
that I was her one-and-only. Reality
was something different. I learned that
the night a man she described as 'just a friend
from college' came to our house and yelled
and pounded on the door she wouldn't open.
Magnetic. A little mean. Impossible to hold.

The truth is my hair is an unworkable tangle.
When she tries to smooth it, I squeal.
Most days I'm rumpled. I lack the helping gene.
I'm not grateful. I peek through her keyhole
to find what I inherited.

When mother grew less beautiful,
she had her nose fixed. She married again.
After that, she swore there were no more men.
But the men she declared she nothing to do with
still came around. When she was eighty-five,
the door-pounder returned to smile across the kitchen
table at her and share his faulty memories.

When she became wide-hipped and irascible,
she threw shoes, screamed at her nurses.
From the sixth-floor psych ward, she vowed
"I'm going to live forever," and I half-believed her.
I was watching even then to discover
what it meant to be a woman, her daughter.

Wendy Taylor Carlisle

The Carnival of the Animals

He follows the link to a YouTube recording
> *Her breath comes in brief rattles;*
and finds he is listening to Spiegel im Spiegel;
> *red raw rage smites her cooper*
a sublime passage by Arvo Pärt,
> *when his hoops round her breasts*
not The Carnival of the Animals he seeks.
> *are shared with a neighbour*
He needs the narrative that lurks behind
> *to give him relief with rutting.*
the raw emotion of her poem.

The titles were not helpful: the first one red,
> *Her face is suffused, riven to rags,*
then rage, and finally revenge
> *deceived by his fickle affection:*
that does not reveal the animal behaviour
> *she feels her throat threshed*
of the East End gang when they caught
> *by the flail of her reaper*
his partner. The fight, the violation,
> *as her red haze rends him ragged.*
the escape at the cost of flashbacks.

He hears the relentless beat of the piano,
> the tears torn from him.
The tune from the cello strings
> that acts as releasing balm:
the fact that men and women
> do not always behave as animals.

Richard Carpenter

The Wise Man

His face now rests far from his Hausa brethren
on an English mantle;
far from the Sahara trade routes which linked his God
across the desert.

Carved from hard, dark wood with rustic strokes,
he sits at ease,
right knee across the other. His hands have settled,
the right rested

on its brother in a mirror pattern. His beard is pointed,
this face at comfort
with his thoughts; his full lips hold a hint at each corner
of a smile.

He has an ample bottom which rests upon a stool;
a round, simple stool
tooled from leather. This firm, stable base supports
his straight back

leading to a pair of shoulders released of tension
with his elbows settled
on his thighs. This posture forms a bowl around his lap
in which he holds

three glass balls: One clear, through which he views
a moonlit night
with clean, fresh air to breathe in. The second, a pale amber
shading into pink

to remind him of an early morning landing at Kano airport
with the vultures circling
on the up-draughts; a landing that he made
by falling gently

from the skies above Tripoli across a cool Sahara
and only knew it
when he saw the palm trees wave a welcome
along the runway.

The third is the blood red warning of a brief Nigerian sunset
before a dense, black night.
A deep, dark red he holds close to his chest to remind him
what to treasure.

Richard Carpenter

Christmas Eve, 2020

They offered us hope
                in the form
of a Christmas bubble
                that burst
as bubbles tend to do.

So now you sit at home, alone,
            the corner of your living room
lit sparsely by a Christmas tree
                barely five feet tall
            and a little worse for wear.

We learned from your resilience,
    your successes and mistakes,
            adding our own
        to complete the picture

like the sun-damaged photographs
            littering the windowsill
        your eyes are struggling to see

        and the boxes of slides
between the piles of magazines
        full of people and places
you remember a little more slowly
        every time you look at them.

            I picture your smile
        as you sing to yourself
        the root notes of a carol,

knowing the cross
this year
        will stand
                unaccompanied
                by your voice.

Joseph Chaplin

On Finding I Still Want You

They made a measure of magnitude,
a system for calculating brilliance
a human notion, if ever –
starlight, rated in numbers, invisible rungs on a skyward ladder like
marks doled out to worthy schoolchildren,
reaching reaching reaching.

So that
if A called out to B,
stretching long stardusty fingers across
eons of night staked with light
to forge some cosmic tethered tin-can telephone – *guess who?* –
the echo down the line
of you of us of wanting
might be the answer –
the most brilliant.

But it's been dial-tone dark here for years.

To think that now
that swallowed starlight you've long tended there,
in the egg cups behind your eyelids,
could flare again, for me, hatching
in this
unassuming suburban space
overstuffed and disparate with so much
uncharged detritus
– tasseled throw pillows, that braided rug I never liked, a dying fern –
seems almost cruel:

A silly wink from a Janus-faced moon,
all glancing eyelashes and lunar curls,
apple-cheeked from chuckling at the specks of us,
butting along on a course not of our making,
unless it is.

Because here you are,
with only feet but also light-years (and the fern)
separating us,
each held gaze a signal fire
a torch passed

an ignition,
quickening a heat I hadn't known lay
coiled in my dragon belly, still.

I could just say, *It's nice to see you again.*
It's been a while.
I could offer you iced tea and fan myself.

But fire knows only to consume
and I have always liked the diesel taste of you.
And starlight, even hemmed,
is made for dancing.

I don't know if it's true,
what they say about fireflies
glowing just to die — a call left unanswered.
But I know today, standing on the unloved braided rug,
I feel like burning.

Allison Collins

Family Entertainment Sixties Style

We are watching a complicated thriller on our unpredictable monochrome TV. The main suspect, a young woman, is getting out of a conjugal bed very quietly. Meanwhile, in the garden shadows, a man who may be a detective turns to his companion, opens his mouth to whisper, and Dad says "Isn't that what's-his-name, the one who does impersonations, you know..." Mum and I pretend not to hear, but now we have missed a vital piece of dialogue half a century before replay and catch-up. The woman puts on her dressing gown and goes down to the living room. The men who may or may not be detectives are watching. Dad says "You know, Derek, David, Donald..." I do know. I know the actor's name, his wife's name, and roughly how old he is, which will be what Dad comments on next, as he quaffs his notorious home-made damson wine. Mum and I sip his wine very slowly. It undermines my grip on the plot, but Mum seems to be able to keep up (possibly because, every now and then, she tips a bit into the tradescantia). Dad says "This reminds me of..." He names some obscure film from the Forties which he has probably never actually seen. I am seething with fourteen-year-old rage. A murder is about to be committed, and not necessarily on screen. Mum senses it. She says to Dad "Do you think you had better check on Gran?" Dad points vaguely at the screen. He says "How much longer does this thing go on?" "Five weeks" says Mum "I think Gran called." Snowflakes cross the screen horizontally. Dad gets up unsteadily and thumps the top of the TV hard. The picture disappears altogether but the sound continues. "What are you doing down here" asks the husband, who was obviously not as asleep as his wife had hoped. Dad disappears behind the set to twiddle knobs at random. "I was just..." The sound goes and the picture returns. The husband catches sight of a movement in the garden and mouths something. The wife looks out of the French windows and mouths something back, with a shrug. Dad misses all this because he is still twiddling behind the set. The sound suddenly returns, extremely loud. Mephistopheles (our cat) runs up the curtains in terror, perches on the rail and hisses at us with bared teeth. I leave the room in search of biscuits, anything.

Nigel Collins

33

Young Elizabethans

We snip-snapped our folded paper fortune-tellers,
knuckles raw from conker miss-hits.
We played for keeps with half-alleys, bloods, swirls and pewits.
We clung to ledges until our fingers gave way and we were tagged.
Lead soldiers floated down on hankie parachutes
while we strafed them with gravel.
We were outlaws, spies, tribal warriors, and spacemen.

We couldn't know the meadows were doomed
when we crouched in long grasses watching
iridescent beetles, spindly translucent harvestmen,
spittlebugs feeding in their blankets of foam,
and the crash-landings of blundering cockchafers.
When we stood we startled sudden bright clouds of butterflies.

To shirk adults we built dens or hid
in the upper branches of trees.
We lurked in the voids between bombed buildings
or among spiders and mice in disused dug-outs.
We wrote pointless secret messages with lemon juice ink.

We wanted to break bounds, to create, to revel, to be amazed;
to unravel what came before the beginning or
how fast you must travel to cheat time.

We were creatures spawned, fed, watered, inoculated, and inculcated
by maimed, bereaved, and shell-shocked mentors.
We were drilled to salute their god, their flag, and the new queen.
While we transcribed highfalutin Latin phrases with dip pens
we were led to believe that poverty was just bad luck.

We played in our little safe havens while
hedges were grubbed, forests felled, and rivers stifled.
We stumbled on blinded rabbits with hideous faces
groping in the margins of poisoned fields.
We glimpsed our nation shrivelling and warping
in the grip of arrogant and incompetent leaders
armed with cataclysmic weaponry.

We were hailed as special and precious;
a generation who had never had it so good;
who were told "You are the future,
we have done all this for you."

Nigel Collins

The Theory of Everything

The distant swell we tip to break big
collides with a rollback
sucks itself in and
fizzles.
We guess wrong wave after wave.

Moon and wind riffle and shake out the sea's mantle
until it frays white along the strand
where we make it doomed channels and dams,
or flirt with the tide thigh deep
shrieking like gulls.

There are patterns to the rollers that may be rules
but we don't know them all
and are still made fools by floods
from which we never learn enough;
or by that forty ninth surge
while posing cocksure on a slimy rock.

Mostly we just bob in the shallows
on a slowly deflating airbed
squinting at the sky
as if we can read messages in clouds.

Nigel Collins

Right at the edge

Right at the edge she was,
staring down at the sea.

That tall woman,
I never see her teeth when she talks.
Melissa she said, *Melissa.*

The girl took no notice so she made this huge stride,
it looked a bit funny but she wasn't being funny
and locked her arm through the girl's skin and bone

then steered her so she had to turn.
The girl didn't mind
just kept staring back at the sea.

Thrift was dangling
dried up pompoms on wavy stalks
like bits of electrics.

As soon as they were back on the path the girl bolted,
leaping over nettles with no shoes or socks on

and there was this man there,
really hairy arms, who said *well she's alright.*

Pamela, that's her name, Pamela smiled –
a hundred and eighty-degree curse

then saw me coming so I put Oblong's lead on.
Good evening, I called. *What a lovely day it's been.*

She looked at me as if I were a talking frog
but I got away, thank God.

Annemarie Cooper

Black Roots

My hair is black striped against yellow —
Dirty barcodes.
I run my fingers through and they
Race in separate lanes.
I free my hair from the elastic and shake it down.
It is long but flat as cigarette paper
Pinching my skin as it hangs —
My only refuge of the feminine.
I have nothing else to show, nothing which
Adorns me.
I am naked.
I stand, looking downwards, a priest at the pulpit.
My stomach rolls in, under and over itself sumptuously like sand dunes.
You ask me to move my hair out of the way.
I used to pray that you would not judge me but you're
Not — you're looking at me.
The whole lot of it.

Charlotte Cosgrove

Fantasy Addiction

I have an addiction to fantasy.
I am a celebrity dating another celebrity.
That man coming out of the shop is my long lost father.
I have won an Oscar, a Pulitzer, a Grammy
And my personal favourite: a Nobel Prize
For absolutely anything.
I have won Miss World with my glowing complexion,
My supple chest and proclamation of world peace.
All this whilst simultaneously opening and running
A homeless shelter, single-handedly.
I am the detective in the movie who always cracks the case,
The best singer in the whole musical,
The millionaire with the good heart.
And like all good fantasies I try to cling on
Too hard, so tight it crushes —
Tiny pieces of different lives all over the floor.
And it is my job to sweep them all up,
Try to piece the remnants together.

Charlotte Cosgrove

In the Realm of Hungry Ghosts

I lie in my love-nest of captured light fragments
(one of the worst things of mine) to find peace.
Collected by the riverbed, the highway, the sea.

Poe, Bronte, and Maso mock me from the wall,
listening to that
"what-may-have-been" song.
You can't remember how it goes because you haven't heard it before.

Pressed far into this ground,
not much of a home.
It will suck you dry.
You'll mistake it for a heat tremor.
Sore, pink and purple shoulders from forcing it.

I want only, only
full acceptance of that towering slab from which I came.

That truth or deep belief you both share.
Its own language in stone, somewhere along the lines of,
"can't believe we made it this far."

If I quit now I could live another 2.8 years.
Counting them as inches on my waist,
as if I were a tree.

"Here was a year of plentiful water."
Much like judging the worth of a fruit by its weight.
Should it be past ripe, (cue the Optimist)
it can feed the barn sparrow above my door.

Erin Davis

All Hallows

Her face is a smudged sketch
in the mirror's grey sheen,
her hair crackles as she brushes,
sweeping down from crown to breast.
Stars flicker in the glass.

Moonlight sets shadow bars
across her untidy bed,
it stripes her pillow,
her tumbled sheet.

The door opens,
behind her, the darkness ripples,
her mirror dims.
A step whispers on the carpet.

The door clicks shut.

Afterwards
she is a stone
clenched tight
against the bare skull-face
leering at the window

An owl shrieks.

Sara Davis

The Farmer's Wife

Marred by work and time, the farmer
bends slowly down the sheep-tufted hill,
eyed by his stone-faced ewes.
Above him, ragged crows wheel and mock.
From the unlit house, his wife watches
his shadow lengthen. She
presses her white, moth face to the window
to see the bright-headed ploughboy
open the black earth in rhythmic curves.

The kitchen is sweet with baking,
she grasps the heavy, silver knife,
slices the golden sponge, precisely.
She stirs sugar, fine, white granules,
into his tar-brown tea; waits, patient,
while the brisk, fish life leaps within her.
The door swings wide, she makes a smile for him
as the wind gusts in, ripe with tilth.
Outside, the ploughboy lingers, hoping
to glimpse her secret spark.

Sara Davis

a life at sea

born without anchor
you always had far to go
slave to an eternal current
that swept you away on an endless journey

you always had far to go
prisoner to an implacable mistress
that swept you away on an endless journey
searching for the bedrock of you

prisoner to an implacable mistress
a shapeshifter with no home port
searching for the bedrock of you
cursed with the fate of unplanned

a shapeshifter with no home port
slave to an eternal current
cursed with the fate of the unplanned
born without an anchor

R C de Winter

Self-portrait in the Pointillist Fashion

You sit, viewing the painting from a bench
across the room. She squints, nose as close to
the canvas as the velvet ropes allow. Its paint is

a gesture that entrances, the table in this lower
corner a crowd of yellow, red, purple. Even now,
she senses the brown they form. But this close,

the reds are larger than the yellow, and the weave
of the canvas shows between the individual dabs.
They cluster like hexagon cells arranged in a honeycomb,

the place of primal industry. Yet there still is room
between each cell, where the space of adjacency gestures
towards the infinite space we fall into, unable to arrive

at our destinations. These cells buzz with their
common purpose. No gathering, but no escape.
Eventually, she will return to you – still sitting

across the gallery – you a room away, staring
at the painting across the distance, lamenting every
inch of that distance. *From here, there's a narrative,*

answers, the promise of unity, you say. And your words
break off. Later at the café, you stir the cinnamon specks
on your latte into the foam, your own tawny mix.

She reaches across the table. You sit straight,
not bending to touch her stretched arm. Always the space
of cells apart. You're too busy gazing at others

eating their Sunday lunch; you never noticed her gesture.

Andrea Jane Dickens

Apples Today

Arrive airfreighted to table from Tesco,
not often enough from our greengrocer,
and hardly ever from a local garden.

What a precious gift when a friend
shows up with a bag of freshly picked
fruit and veg, and insists that you cook

or eat all of it, and asks what you will create,
then goes on her way without waiting for
the invite to dinner, but you know she will

remind you later, just to make sure you are
looking after yourself, and of course you do
not want to disappoint your compañera,

so you will slice then fry the courgettes
in olive oil, and parboil the runner beans,
and use up every potato before they soften,

and you will eat one of her apples every day,
because they are good, and not just because
she told you they are an old Sussex variety

you cannot buy, and yes, you forgot to ask
their name, but you will remember their taste,
and tell her how they rounded off your meals.

Brian Docherty

Errata

(Remembering Larry Tesler, creator of cut, copy, paste, and search for the computer)

Could I call back anything, I'd
take back suspicions, invective,
any sin or scepter I had to hide,
and clear my way to live,
trying to uncover and replant
whatever I'd coveted and gained,
but this time erase the giant
ego trips, the soiled, the stained,
and put them in their proper place
to be hidden again, never found.
I'd smooth scripted wrinkles from my face
and suture my soul into the ground.

William Dubie

Eligible Upgrade

"Finally, I'm eligible for an upgrade. Time to get a new phone," I said from the depths of my couch.

"Oh, honey," wearily sighed my current cell phone, "you'll never be able to replace me." She paused as her chunky frame was wracked by a sudden spasm of hacking coughs; in a flurry, one app after another glitched across her touch screen, the camera opening for a brief moment to reflect my skeptical visage from the most unflattering angle under my chin. "They don't make models like me anymore," she determined, her voice phlegmy and ragged.

"Yeah, I hope not," I chuckled, "you're six years old, Gladys. You're totally obsolete."

"Whoa, hold on there, hon," Gladys cautioned. Her screen flashed an alarming shade of red. "I think you're forgetting what we've been through together. How many times have ya' dropped me in the mud? How many times have I been in the room when ya' having sex? And I never complain."

I crossed my arms. "Three and five," I said, flatly, "and you complain *all* the time. Besides, you know I'm not that active, don't try and throw *that* in my face."

I levered myself from the sunken couch cushions and plodded across the living room to the door, slipping on my black running sneakers and grey, quilted hoodie with a shrug.

"Whadda 'bout the cost then, huh?" Gladys prodded, "They charge an arm and a leg for those shiny new models and ya' know what? I betcha they'll break just from ya' breathing on 'em."

I patted my pants for my wallet and keys before opening the door to my apartment, stepping out onto the concrete stoop and locking it behind me. I slid my phone into my left cheek pocket and moved towards my car.

"Not like me, honey!" shouted Gladys, muffled by the denim, "I've been with ya' six years and look at me! Not a crack!"

"Yeah," I muttered softly, unlocking the driver's side door to my old, silver Volvo, "that's 'cause I bought a nice case for you and have replaced your damn screen protector like three times."

The Volvo started with a splutter; while I allowed it to warm up for a couple seconds, I retrieved my phone from my pocket and attempted to load up my music app. It took a minute and a half to open, the loading wheel in the center of the screen spinning endlessly as Gladys tried to reason with me.

"Okay, well think about that then, hon," she said evenly, "ya' gonna have to buy a whole new case and charger and—" she stuttered briefly as

I plugged in the audio jack, "—and converters. Ya' gonna have to buy all new audio converters for ya' car and speakers and headphones and whatnot."

"Well, you know what?" I said as I reversed from the parking spot in my apartment complex, "It's a small price to pay for a phone whose screen doesn't randomly open apps or press buttons I didn't want pressed. You know, like 'liking' my ex's photos or swiping right on that coworker of mine I definitely didn't want to start shit with." I merged into traffic, beginning my journey to the phone store. "Not to mention the dropped calls and butt dials, laggy texting and *super* limited storage."

Gladys' lock screen darkened, begrudgingly. "But I ain't broke though."

After parking in the cramped lot and migrating in through the sliding doors, I discovered the phone store to be sparsely populated, minimalistic in design and whiter than the inside of a bleach bottle. As soon as I stepped across the threshold, one of the blue-polo clad attendants hurried up to me.

"What's your purpose here today?" He inquired in a high falsetto. He was a heavy set, bald, ginger-bearded man whose name tag proclaimed him to be, 'Rudy.'

"I, um, I'm here to upgrade my phone," I managed in reply.

"Are you eligible?" Rudy asked.

"Yes, I'm eligible," I answered.

Rudy waved me on with one of his freckled forearms. "Alrighty then," he said happily, "follow me and we'll get you all set up." He led me into the back left corner of the phone store's starship-like interior, gesturing for me to take a seat at a tall, round table. With a tablet in hand, Rudy took the other seat. Tapping at the screen, he glanced up and inquired about my phone number.

"Don't tell me ya' gonna transfer my number—my digits!—over to some round-edged punk!" Gladys gasped with horror. I held her in my clenched hand on the tabletop.

"Shhh!" I hissed sharply at my phone.

"Excuse me?" asked Rudy, furrowing his brow, "I just asked for your phone number...?"

"Yeah, sorry," I mumbled, embarrassed and gave him my number.

"The indecency," Gladys croaked.

"Okay, here you are," Rudy stated, pulling up my account information. "You are indeed eligible. Let's see what your options are." With deft swipes at his tablet he pulled up a catalog menu, displaying four options for me to choose from.

"So, this is what your plan covers, upgrade-wise," he said, "depending on your needs, you can choose from the KY-13," he pointed to a boxy, silver model with one centrally-located camera lens. "Or the MEG-1N," a glossy black phone with a curved profile and two massive camera lenses in its left corner. "The N-8T was just reduced in price, that's a popular, well-rounded model," Rudy continued, thumbing at a picture of a soft-edged charcoal grey device, also with two lenses but more moderately sized, and a decent waterfall display. "And finally, the L-1Z, it's a favorite with mobile-gamers—has one of the newest processors." The last phone was white and giant; it had six camera lenses clustered in its right corner, yet still had enough room on its dinner-plate sized profile to get a firm, two-handed grip.

"Punks! Every single one of them, punks!" shouted Gladys from my clenched hand. "I'm telling ya', hon," she scolded, "they'll crack—they'll break right away, hon, I'll guarantee it. Not a single one of 'em could last as long as I have!"

I considered the four options proffered before me for a silent moment before asking, "Which one do you think is the most durable? Like, which will last the longest?"

Rudy leaned forward, tilting his head so he could examine the tablet he held, upside down. "Hmm," he pondered, "Well, to tell the truth, these are all pretty new models; so, I don't know for sure. But if you're looking for the best bang for your buck for just normal phone usage, the N-8T is the most well-rounded."

I considered a moment longer, flitted my eyes back and forth between the four models; I inspected the different features, the abundance of camera lenses, the general aesthetics (which, admittedly, would soon be masked by a case). I hissed a puff of air through my teeth and pointed at the third option.

"I'll go for the best bang for my buck I guess," I decided.

"Okay, great, I'll go grab that." Rudy tapped the table, indicated that he'd, "...be right back," and departed behind a cream-tinted sliding door that made a pleasing *whooshing* sound as it rolled shut.

"N-8T..." spat Gladys, "what sort of useless model is that POS?"

"Can you just cool it?" I quietly asked, exhausted. "You had to know this day was gonna come eventually. You're lucky that I haven't replaced you sooner." I rubbed at my brow, my elbows resting on the laminated surface of the tall table.

"Honey," Gladys said, " Us G106-Y5s are built to last. We don't expect anything but to work and work and work. I'm still in my prime."

"That's hilarious," I scoffed, "do phones in their prime randomly uninstall apps I'm in the middle of using?"

"What's that?" Rudy the attendant's sibilant tones inquired, re-approaching the table with a slim, white box in his hands.

"Nothing," I hurriedly replied, "uh, just thinking aloud." I hadn't heard him come back through the sliding door, but—as if to deny my bewilderment—the *whoosh* of it closing was audible all the same.

Rudy shrugged and sat across from me at the table once more. From the slim, white box he pulled a pristine, immaculately clean, charcoal grey model N-8T phone out and placed it screen-up on the tabletop. Then, he stretched a hand out to me.

"Can I have your old phone?" he asked, "I'll transfer your number and once we get you a case, you can be on your way."

"Oh. Yeah, sorry, of course," I stammered and moved to hand him my phone. However, I hesitated for a brief moment, appraising Gladys and her chunky profile—her cramped screen and all the glitches she contained —for the last time. Six years was a long time to spend with anything, let alone something that had spent all two thousand, one hundred and sixty days going *everywhere* with me. I couldn't remember the last time I'd taken a crap without Gladys. I shook myself from my reverie and handed Rudy the phone.

"Okay, here we go," Rudy muttered. Quickly, he shed Gladys of her old, much worn case.

"The indecency!" she cried.

Rudy's sausage-like fingers danced across the surface of his tablet before diverting their attention back to Gladys for a brief moment, pulling up the settings screen. Like a man possessed, Rudy flicked his eyes between his tablet, Gladys and the new N-8T phone with warp speed; his digits danced and his breath came in short, sour cream and onion-scented pants.

"And the transfer has started," Rudy said, finally leaning back, "it'll take a couple minutes for your old phone to be deactivated and for your new phone to turn on."

"No...it's happening, I can already feel it," Gladys whispered from beside the attendant's tablet. I couldn't take my eyes off of her. "So, this is how our relationship dies, with a stranger's greasy fingers all over me." She moaned and let out a long, rattling cough. "Please," she begged, her voice weakening with every word, "what about all the good times? What about that time I started recording when you were getting out of the shower and clipped it to your DMs?"

I struggled to repress welling tears in my eyes. "That wasn't a good time," I murmured.

Gladys coughed raggedly. "It was for me, hon. It was for me..." Her voice trailed off, fading into the ether.

"Gladys?" I whispered, stricken. A lone tear crawled down my cheek, dripping off of my chin and into my lap with a soft *plop*. After a shaky breath, I looked up to realize that Rudy was regarding me with a cocked eyebrow and wide eyes.

"Are you okay, man?" he hesitantly asked.

I sniffed, wiped at my face with the grey sleeve of my hoodie and nodded. "Yeah, sorry," I managed. "She was a horrible phone."

Rudy opened his mouth as if to reply but was saved by a metallic *ding* from his tablet. "Oh, wow. Okay," he said instead. He cleared his throat before continuing, "That was a fast transfer. Your new phone is ready."

I nodded in reply and, seeming to notice my sudden reticence, Rudy added as an afterthought, "Hey, you know, maybe that means this model will be better."

"Yeah, maybe. Thanks, man," I said.

In an awkward silence, Rudy proceeded to process the upgrade and ring up the case I picked out and sent me on my way with my new phone and accessories in an oversized plastic bag and an obligatory, "Have a good day." I hadn't replied, instead opting to hurry from the store before I could witness the shell of a phone that had been Gladys, being tossed into the recycling.

The walk back to my silver Volvo felt like a stroll across the moon: nearly weightless. No chiding. No second guessing—my new phone remained quiet. Maybe the N-8T could prove to be a better model after all.

When I settled into my car, I decided that I wanted to put on some music; something exciting and high energy to celebrate the new era I had just stepped into (and, as well, to dispel the dredges of remorse for my former electronic companion). My music app loaded almost instantaneously and, after plugging in my new converter—which had been *way* too expensive—I jacked my brand new phone into my car stereo and proceeded to play one of my favorite EDM tracks.

"Oh wow, I love this song. Great choice, bud," said a new voice. It sounded pleasant and upbeat, like that of a supportive older brother.

I took my hand away from the Volvo's ignition, shifting my attention to the newly awoken N-8T phone resting on the passenger seat. I couldn't help but raise my eyebrows in surprise—I had expected the refractory period to last a little longer.

"Well, hello," I said, picking up the glossy charcoal-tinted device to better introduce myself.

"Hey, bud, I'm Nate. I'm excited to be your new phone!"

"Hey, Nate. I'm excited to have a new phone," I replied.

"Awesome! I'm downloading all your info from the cloud right now, any particular apps you want right away, bud?" Nate asked, earnest in his desire to serve.

"Wow, uhhh," I said, taken aback, "I guess, uh, just make sure my music, photos and fitness tracker are all installed for now." My initial surprise at Nate's quick awakening was compounded drastically by the sheer novelty of his genuine attempt to be helpful; it was a sensation I was unused to.

"Good call, bud! I can do that." Nate paused for a fraction of a second before continuing in his warm tones, "I see your tracker has data for your last couple runs, those are some good times, bud!"

I couldn't help but smile, pleased by the flattery. "Thanks."

"Of course, bud! Only calling it like I see it."

I adjusted myself in the driver's seat of my Volvo, accidentally catching the glare of the sun in Nate's shiny touch screen and momentarily blinded myself. Blinking the spots from my eyes, I heard Nate make the approximation of clearing his throat and say observantly, "It appears you're about to be on the road, bud. Would you like me to turn on Do Not Disturb until we're home?"

Still with eyes squinched exaggeratedly, my smile widened; my old phone had never once asked that. "Yes, thank you, Nate. I'd appreciate that." I felt a tear sliding out of my left eye; whether from the sun's glare or Nate's honest attentiveness, I couldn't say.

"Sure thing, bud, 'happy to help. Now, I'll let you get back to your commute and your music." Nate's voice ticked upwards happily before he drifted into silence, allowing the EDM song to once more swell through my boxy sedan, unimpeded. Gently, I placed my new phone back onto the passenger's seat cushion and started up my old Volvo.

Willow J Fields

Circus, Versailles

Familiar, sure-footed dance –
pavane, bourrée, and minuet
in candle-light and mirror-glance;
as if they stepped on foot-prints set
upon the floor where they advance.

Perfume and powdered wigs, silk hose,
brocade and buckled shoes: like dolls
they dance attendance and they pose
amongst the curlicues and scrolls
of etiquette, side-stepping toes.

A pattern in their days, embossed
like paper: court intrigues, bedding
so-and-so's mistress, gossip tossed
like knives, though always treading
softly, carefully. They are so lost,

so far inside an intricate
machine, the foot-prints of the dance
become a trail they follow late
into the night. Hope is a chance
that they will not obliterate

a way back out, beyond the pale
of their decorum. On the floor,
they toe their steps like braille,
think of something sharp to feel more
real, say it out loud. And the trail

goes nowhere new and brings them back
to dance in their tight-fitting shoes.
Long mirrors watch them as they rack
themselves wittily, as they lose
all sense of what it is they lack.

Jim Friedman

Oscar's apologia for his Lives

Soon each orifice will explode.
My biographers will note that,
and also when I bit my hand
standing outside a pastry shop,
hungry and mouse-poor in Paris.

Forgive the touches of pathos
and grotesquerie writers make
of my adventures these last years;
they need pepper to season them
and tears to salt my final act.

Yes, men have stared, pointed at me
accusingly for so long now,
I have become my own last play;
a melodrama, perhaps, but
with such a charming leading man.

I play a beggar, cap in hand
held out for notoriety,
praise, fame; most abjectly – it seems
the scribblers want to say – for love
of one incapable of love.

The heart is a bit of a dog,
I think, all too readily
wagging its tail but loyal, too,
once it finds a master, a home
to give and give itself away.

Mine wagged its tail and I found out
how capable I was of being
recklessly, gloriously alive.
And selfish, I admit. But tell me,
why would they have it otherwise?

Scribblers put us on pedestals
and perpetrate idolatries.
Such treasons cannot have enough
enjoyment of the good times,
of spicy downfalls to disgrace.

My farewell after bitter scenes,
trying to keep some dignity
in the gutter – an achievement
I hesitate to recommend –
was the best scene I never wrote.

Jim Friedman

The Leaving of Dermot Burke

Catherine Gallagher sat at a kitchen table in a snug, two-bedroom house in the west of Ireland, outside a town with the ungainly name of Gort. She watched autumn rain slide down a window that carried a spider crack along one edge. It seemed larger than the day before and Catherine wondered if it needed tape to last the winter.

She drank a cup of Barry's Gold Blend tea as she looked out on her garden, sodden and disheveled. Catherine's daughter-in-law, a woman named Maura, had just now asked did she *know a boy growing up named Dermot Burke?*

Catherine was a graceful woman, tall and calm, white-haired and thin, whose smiles were engaging, if sparse. She did indeed recall Dermot Burke, vividly in fact, and was pleased at the recollection of his name, long left unspoken.

I do remember him, she said. *I remember him well. He left for America when I was fifteen. He was older than me by a few years.*

My, that was a long time ago. Maybe the middle thirties, which sounded like 'turties' in her way of saying it. *I was fifteen, so that would make it 1936. I missed him, after he left.*

Catherine at ninety-two, was blessed with a memory that was both cogent and fulsome when allowed to unfold in its own good time. Her daughter-in-law often noted that Catherine's math skills bettered her own.

I was told he went to Detroit and worked in an automobile factory, making cars I suppose. I'm not sure which one; it may have been Henry Ford. We did not hear much about him after he left.

Catherine well knew Dermot had gone to work at Ford, in a town called Highland Park that was surrounded by Detroit; everyone in Gort knew that. His parents mentioned with some pride how he sent money home every month. Few details about Dermot's American life were certain, but that one was. Catherine did not know how much or how little to say about him. Being a private person had served her well in life.

Dermot never came back, you know, she told Maura, *not even when his parents died or little Anya, his sister. She died before they did. Scarlet fever, I'm told. She was ten. Such a sweet thing she was, with her dark, curly hair; dark, dark hair. It was going around, you see, the scarlet fever. Little Anya was not the only one who died.*

Why do you ask about Dermot?

Well, said Maura, *do you remember my friend, Orla? She works at the Lady Gregory Hotel and one of the guests is a man named Bartholomew Burke. He told Orla that Dermot Burke was his father and wondered if there might be anyone in Gort who still remembered the family?*

She thought of you and called me and I called you and here we are. She smiled.

Maura was fond of Catherine. She knew her quirks and had the patience to wait for a reply.

The thing of it is, said Catherine, *this boy Dermot Burke was not of very good reputation. He wasn't a bad boy. He didn't steal or drink too much and get into fights, but he was lusty. He was a good looking lad, you see. The girls liked him.*

They liked his attention. He knew how to talk to a girl. He didn't brag like so many young men. He listened. He was a marvellous listener.

❋ ❋ ❋

A smile crossed Catherine Gallagher's lips, a smile so brief her daughter-in-law missed it. Catherine remembered with utter clarity a chance meeting more than seventy years ago, no more than a chat really, on a country lane with a handsome, older boy, just the two of them.

She was on her way home from the dress shop where she worked after school. Perhaps it was not a chat; perhaps it was a passing conversation. But they were alone, the two of them, and she remembered him asking, *How are you this fine evening?,* touching her bare forearm as they stopped in the road.

I'm fine, said Catherine. *Now I'm better than fine,* pleased at her boldness, at the way she had given her own broad smile in reply.

Is that the truth now? Dermot said. *And where are you off to?*

They talked a bit more, about unimportant things. Then this strong-looking, young man with his easy ways leaned closer to Catherine and kissed her gently on the lips. It was a soft kiss, a kiss without passion, a kiss that said hello young lady. Perhaps he held it longer than he should have for such a kiss and she let him hold that kiss a moment too long, that kiss that had lingered for decades with Catherine Gallagher, who well remembered her long life's moments, good and bad.

They turned away at the same time, laughing at each other, Catherine's cheeks a sudden pink. The young man took four strides down the road and half turned to wave goodbye, to see if Catherine was looking back. She knew better.

She waited until the bend, where the road rolls right, before glancing over one shoulder. Dermot Burke had slipped away.

Catherine Gallagher well remembered that lush spring evening when she was fifteen and Dermot Burke gave her a first kiss on the lips and she was glad she let him.

Even yet, she had told no one but Siobhan, and that was decades ago.

❋ ❋ ❋

To Maura, Catherine said, *He talked to me sometimes, but he wasn't interested in me in a real way. Not pretty enough, I suppose. He was a handsome lad. People said he was lazy because he did not do well in school. That was not true.*

He was a smart one, with a great wit. My mother kept an eye on Dermot. She used old words when she talked about him. She would say to me, 'Don't mind his plámásing.'

And what does it mean? asked Maura.

Plámásing? Flattery, said Catherine. *My mother, God rest her, was telling me to be careful of his words, his way with words. She knew I should watch out for this boy, but she warned me with a smile. She liked him. Most everyone did.*

His attention went to Siobhan O'Connell. Everyone said she was the prettiest girl in the west of Ireland, like Mary Hynes, pursued by the blind poet Raftery. Maybe it was true.

She was a pretty one; that's what got him into trouble. And her. O dear yes, she got into trouble too, didn't she? That's what got them both into trouble. Dermot Burke was lusty and Siobhan was too, I suppose, although you wouldn't know it to talk to her. She was a shy one she was, a sweet girl.

We don't really know people do we? And not when they're young and they don't know themselves at all, not who they are or who they'll be, from one minute to the next.

❊ ❊ ❊

Catherine Gallagher was disinclined to tell Maura about what happened to Siobhan O'Connell, the girl Dermot Burke impregnated so many years ago, before he fled Ireland for America's Upper Midwest and left Siobhan on her own, shunned by the Church, her family shamed, taken by her parents one late Tuesday afternoon in June to a place called St. Mary's Mother and Baby Home in Tuam, thirty-five miles away.

Catherine wanted to visit Siobhan but had no way to get to the home and no way back and never did go. Besides, her parents forbade it. Siobhan's parents visited once, *after the baby was born and sold off.* That's the way Catherine always thought of it, that the baby was *sold off by the nuns.*

Catherine did not want to talk about her friend's unhappy life. Dermot Burke was not a bad man, but he did some bad things. *He was a coward, wasn't he? And a scoundrel,* she said unwittingly.

Who was? asked Maura.

Instead of an answer Catherine shook her head, unnerved by what she had recalled after so many years of firmly not doing so.

❊ ❊ ❊

It's Dermot Burke's son from America asking after his father, is it? He's here on a visit? In Gort? Come here to me now, she said to Maura. *These were not trifling matters, what Dermot Burke did, what happened to Siobhan O'Connell. I cannot tell this man about his father.*

What would you do if you heard such a story about your own father? And from a stranger? Does this man know about the baby at all? She would be his half sister.

Maura said, *I don't believe he knows much about his father's life in Ireland. That's why he's here, I suppose, to find out more.*

Catherine made a sound of disapproval, sliding her tongue quickly off the roof of her mouth. *Fathering a child out of wedlock is no small sin, and then running off without a word. Ah, no. I won't do it. Amn't I the one who should be worried? No, I won't talk to the son of Dermot Burke about his father. And I'm not sorry about it.*

* * *

Maura visited Catherine two days later, a schedule of visits they had developed over the years. She brought biscuits frosted with caramel and made tea and they sat in the kitchen and looked out the same cracked window to the same sodden garden that waited for spring like the rest of the western world.

Catherine sipped her tea, holding the cup by its handle, her left hand cradling the bottom to capture its warmth. The cup rattled in the saucer when she set it down.

She looked at Maura and said, *Did I mention that I was a good friend of Siobhan O'Connell, the girl who carried Dermot Burke's baby? We wrote each other off and on for some years after she left Gort – no, that's not right. She did not leave Gort. She fled, didn't she? One morning without a word she took the train to Dublin and then off to London.*

Catherine paused, *I've decided to tell you something, Maura.*

Siobhan stopped writing to me because of the past. I think writing to me reminded her of Niamh – that was her baby's name – and that unhappy time. A lot of Irish girls went to London then, for work. It was hard times. She died about six years ago. I don't believe Siobhan ever knew what happened to her child.

Catherine looked at Maura and said in a voice that was steady and quiet, *But I know. I know what happened to little Niamh.*

You do? said Maura, surprised.

A couple from Belfast adopted her. They were wealthy; Catholic of course. The nuns from the home would have it no other way, as if that made things any better. I talk to Niamh quite often. She is now a woman, of course, not as old as I am but not young. But that is not her name now, is it?

A surprised Maura asked, *You talk to Siobhan's child? Recently?*

Yesterday, as a matter of fact.

* * *

Catherine Gallagher finished her tea with a final sip, confident she had Maura's attention.

Shall I go on then?

Maura nodded and leaned forward, her tea lukewarm.

Do you know the house outside town, just off the Clontarf Road? The one near the dairy? Do you know it?

Catherine moved on as if Maura did.

It sold two years ago. Very inexpensive I am told. Such a long time it was empty. I knew that house growing up. Not to visit, but I knew the people who lived there.

One day, the son of that house moved out suddenly, left to work in America. He never returned to Gort or to Ireland or to his family. They had a hard time of it after that. He sent money home but they all died within a few years of his leaving. The house fell to desperate ruin.

No one wanted that house, you see. It went to the bank and the bank held an auction and it was bought and sold over the many years but no one stayed. Renters, I suppose. And then it was – O, what do people call it, that bad housing problem a few years back?

The housing bubble? said Maura.

That's it! The housing bubble. When the housing bubble came to Ireland the house withered and died. It was never home to another living soul. Did you see it?

Maura shook her head no.

Weeds knee high all around, the thatch moldy, rain dripping inside, windows broken. I'm told there were needles on the floor. From drug addicts, I suppose. I didn't know we had such people here. It was a terrible sight.

* * *

Catherine looked past Maura, her eyes unfocused, as if she was watching the unhappy family who once lived in that house, the young man who left abruptly, the father who worked little and talked less, the mother who repaired clothing at the same seamstress shop where Catherine once worked; the daughter who died as a child.

I've been talking to a woman named Helen Patterson, who bought that house, said Catherine. *She found me one day, I'm not sure how, but we began to talk. She's fixed it up. You've seen it, haven't you? It's grand.*

She lives in France, in the south where it's warm, but comes to Ireland in the better weather and stays into the autumn. Maybe you've seen her in town? She helps out at the library; a well dressed woman, friendly. She taught at university in Belfast. Her husband has passed away.

She came to see me and now we visit. We have much in common, you see. Catherine paused and took another sip of her tea and looked over the rim of the cup at Maura.

O yes! said Maura, snapping her fingers. *I do know the house you mean. Yes, it looks wonderful now.*

Catherine nodded. *I think your Mr. Burke should talk to Mrs. Patterson. I think it would be useful for him.*

Maura looked puzzled.

I don't understand, Catherine. Does she know something about Mr. Burke's family, this Mrs. Patterson?

Why Maura, said Catherine, *don't you see, dear? It's Dermot Burke's old house that Mrs. Patterson lives in. The one her father grew up in. Mrs. Patterson is Siobhan's baby, little Niamh, all grown up and with a new name.*

She's your Mr. Burke's half sister, isn't she?

Timothy Kenny

Gardener's Lament

As if October's ending isn't bad enough – nightfall
brought forward by an hour, curtain-closing not long
after lunch – there's that last farewell. From now

there'll be a barren stretch. No more cheerful
Friday greetings from between the cosmos and the dahlias,
no faithful hounds following their master's boots –

Nellie, glossy golden, with her soft brown eyes,
and Patti with spiky hair and stumpy legs, who'll never
take Nigel's place: he was loved by everyone

with his passion for apples and air of grizzled wisdom.
No more Monty in his cotton jacket over cords, braces
defiantly on show, pockets fat with balls of twine,

penknife, hanky, pencil, labels, phone. His hair, a little
thinner now, springs in greying curls often starred
with drops of rain. His knowledge is wide, enthusiasm

endless, encouragement invaluable. He teaches
by example: never covers up his failures or mistakes.
But 'Goodbye' Longmeadow for twenty gloomy weeks.

May the dark months pass swiftly till, in March
he's back, smiling welcome from among narcissi,
crocus and fritillaries, signalling the benison of spring.

Gill Learner

The Hillbilly Shed was next door to the Midwest Mother Road Motel, a renovated icon of Route 66's glory days. If the motel showed at least aspirations to a luxury roadside hotel of the past, the gift shop's decor and products were consciously kitsch. But Janet never omitted a chance to survey its products, even with the Covid-19 virus still spreading.

"Now, this . . . ," she said to Curtis. "*This* I have to have."

The teacup sized, toilet shaped, porcelain ashtray was called "Butt Dump."

"Wait," he insisted. "There are lots more good Show Me products like," he pointed, "the Missouri Weener Kleener" (a block of wood with a hole in it), "the Hillbilly Bank" (a sock), and "the Ozark Boob Kit" (two balloons).

She laughed. "You're right! So hard to choose."

They were members of the Fairfield (Missouri) High School Reunion Planning Committee, which was gathering to research meeting venues, entertainment options, catering services for a belated 50-year celebration. They'd grown up in the same neighborhood and, until recently, saw each other when visiting their parents. Today they were making up for lost chances.

"I'm glad we're the only customers," Janet said. "Nobody in this town wears a mask." They both did.

Curtis agreed. "At the motel last night there was a repeat of the famous Memorial Day Lake of the Ozarks pool party." Pictures of dozens of mask-less vacationers crowded in a swimming pool had gone viral in June. The swimsuit clad partiers became poster children for those who saw the virus as a media and Democratic hoax—until, of course, many later tested positive.

He remembered how he, as a high schooler, had similarly dismissed the chances of his going to Vietnam. But he'd been drafted and spent a year there—at the same time, it turned out, as Janet. He was an Army correspondent, and she was in military intelligence; but they'd never talked about their experiences. This weekend she explained what she'd done in-country; and he added another regret to his time in Vietnam. But she carried, he would learn, far deeper sorrow.

Janet turned back to the shelves she'd been examining. "I love coming in here for the goofiness of it all, but they sometimes have some fine local craft items—braided rugs, knitted shawls, wall hangings."

"Ah, your line of work—weaving." She was a "fabric artist" and offered classes at St Louis University. Someone in the class had sent on a newspaper article explaining how her work was getting new attention these days.

"Not sure I can find the right thing," he said. "But I might look out for a gag gift for Beth." His wife was a retired biology professor, so he started checking out goofy anti-environmental coffee mugs: "Bring back leaded gas" (sign on an outhouse); "Open season on tree-huggers" (Jane Fonda the target); "Recycle your brain" (a trash can).

"I'm going with the Butt Dump," Janet insisted. "We tend to forget that much of our youth was passed in smoke-filled rooms—at home, restaurants, college classrooms. It'll be a not too subtle reminder of human stupidity." She turned it in her hand, inspecting. "And this is actually not badly done." The toilet/ashtray was decorated with flowers in a variety of colors and sizes.

Their generation's parents were smokers, and public facilities and most homes in their day had a least one ashtray. Some commemorated places visited (like Hannibal), events in their lives (25th wedding anniversary), homes of famous people (President Harry Truman). But there were also other the off-color items that had their place in Hillbilly Shed.

Curtis admitted, "My mom smoked, but moderately. Now, my dad…"

"Hey," Janet interrupted, "you remember the little gift package we Army recruits received at induction? They contained gum, a pocket copy of the New Testament, and several miniature packs of cigarettes—was it four smokes in each?"

"Now that you mention it, I do remember. If you didn't 'light 'em up' on the day you went in, you probably did later."

"Tobacco is history in this country," mused Janet. "The industry was powerful. But we have new American vices like fast-foods. People no longer plant gardens, cook, put up fruit and vegetables. It's another of those two steps forward, one step back kind of progress."

"When we had to clear out our parents' home, I was struck by how strongly the smell of tobacco permeated clothes, furniture, and carpets in our old house. I guess it was one of those things we repress about the past."

She gave a thin smile. "We Midwesterners are good at repression."

He picked up another item. "Now this is truly tacky." There was a postcard with the words "Ozar-Key" printed on one side. The back featured the drawing of an outhouse. There was no lock on the door, no key attached.

She shook her head. "It's amazing how America has always been able to generate tacky memorabilia, often mocking our own regional traits."

"Did you ever visit Saigon's black market? It was easy to find, and the venders certainly welcomed GIs."

"Many times, in fact." Janet seemed suddenly pensive, and he raised his eyebrows in a question.

She went on. "It some ways shopping on Tudo Street changed the trajectory of my life."

"I'd like to hear about that, but I don't think the Hillbilly Shed is the best place."

"Let's go somewhere else, though in some ways this *is* the perfect context for the story of who I am today."

She gestured toward the locked case behind the counter where cigarettes were kept. "Don't forget that cigarettes were currency over there. You bought and sold with Marlboros."

"Yes, goods *and* services. Well, we've got time to talk more. Meanwhile, I need to get this." He hold up a slim volume, *Dirt on my Shirt*, a children's book by hillbilly expert, Jeff Foxworthy.

Displayed around the cash register were miniature outhouses, whiskey jugs, and coffee cups picturing buxom girls in pigtails wearing short shorts. Janet and Curtis stood as far back from the sales clerk as they could; but he seemed not to notice their caution or their masks. Curtis was sure the bulge in the man's cheek was chewing tobacco. He guessed there was a can behind the counter he would spit in.

There was also a basket of corncob pipes for sale. Janet pointed and said, "This is another of those 'success stories' that has its dark side. I'll tell you on the way to the park."

He and Janet had decided to go sit on the benches at Westview Park, a famous petting location of their teenage years. It was on a high ridge and offered a westward view of famous Route 66 snaking down toward the Gasconade River.

Curtis knew that Washington, thirty miles west of St. Louis, advertised itself as the "Corn Cob Pipe Capital of the World". As they rode from the Hillbilly Shed through town Janet recited the history of The Missouri Meerschaum Company, "world's oldest and largest manufacturer of corn cob pipes".

Local legend claimed that a Washington resident was the first to carve a pipe bowl out of a corn cob. The friend he offered it to liked it so much that the man moved from woodcarving to pipe production, and an industry was born. "I do like it when a local craft gets recognition," she concluded.

"This one, though, was less craft than cheap manufacturing," Curtis said.

"Correct. But local crafts were what I found in Saigon, the beautiful lacquered frames and the decorated silk tapestries." She paused. "More on that shortly. Now, the corncob pipe industry was a boon economically, but that success expanded the use of tobacco and its effect on the nation's health."

Curtis speculated. "I suspect pipe-making companies supported the tobacco companies whose research showed there were no harmful effects from smoking."

"When some of my grandchildren were experimenting with cigarettes a few years ago," said Janet, "I researched the history. The Surgeon General's report came out soon after we graduated. We all ignored it, even though they printed those warnings on the packages."

"And yet we called cigarettes 'coffin nails'! We managed to keep that bit of wisdom disconnected from ourselves."

"Just as today's college students don't anticipate having the respiratory diseases, the high blood pressure, the liver problems related to smoking."

Curtis agreed "They're lucky that they don't have to anticipate going to war, but they are going to face an international health crisis they didn't see coming."

"Covid-19. No-one but the career epidemiologists foresaw it."

"My wife knows a lot about SARS and other infectious diseases, and some of her former students are on the front line of research."

"That's great. The town of Washington's young men back in the day were making successive improvements in manufacturing and distributing of corn cob pipes, not vaccines or drugs. And that led to as many as a dozen more businesses sending their products around the world. When health scares about cigarettes soared, many smokers switched to pipes, believing them less harmful. So it was more business for Missouri."

Curtis couldn't say how many years pipe smoking had taken off his father's life . . . or how many his own dozen years of smoking—late high school, the Army, and through college—might cost him. In the biographical statements he was receiving about deceased classmates, how many were smokers who died of lung cancer or heart failure?

"So," he asked Janet when they'd settled on a open picnic shelter, "Saigon's black market changed your life?"

"Ah, yes. I'd done a lot of research on the system—part of my intelligence assignment, in fact. There was subtle cooperation among American businesses, transportation companies, and quartermaster units that leaked goods into the streets of major South Vietnamese cities. I had a virtual catalog of products being bought, sold, bought again."

"Ha, you could have opened up a GI Hillbilly Shed over there! Made a mint."

"Almost. What began to interest me, though, were the items traditionally made by the Vietnamese themselves—clothes and pottery, for instance."

"I remember that there were little shops on the big bases. GI's could buy tea sets and ao dais to ship back to girlfriends or mothers. Although I never bought anything, the businesses—like the Chinese restaurants and the bowling alleys—reminded me that life in the rear was radically different from the bush. Grunts spent their money on beer and women."

"And, as you'd expect, the goods at those little shops were tailored— pun intended—to American tastes. On the black market, I found, you could find more authentic products. I went there with . . . with my boyfriend of the time."

"Not the man you married, though, right?"

"No. In fact, he was one of those who survived the war but not the peace. Anyway, I guess that's one of the reasons I remember the black market so well."

Curtis had nothing to say.

"Another reason that time was critical for me is that I met a woman there, a refuge from the North who was surviving by decorating metal cigarette lighters, a favorite purchase of Americans."

"Ah, makes sense, sadly. Every soldier had one."

"She could paint the standard WWII airplane pinups, Navy anchors and Army guns, hearts with arrows through them. To stay on at a cheap hotel, though, she had to meet a daily quota."

"Must have been painstaking work."

"It was sweatshop labor, in fact. I'd learned enough Vietnamese, and she English, that I could sit and talk with her as she worked—so long as I always bought something and she kept to her deadlines. After a number of visits—and purchases—I asked about her past, whether she'd had any training. And, in fact, she'd studied in Beijing after schooling in the North."

"But she wasn't painting cigarette lighters in China and her home country."

"No, traditional Vietnamese lacquered frames and porcelain dishes. She was," she chuckled, "also a weaver."

"Ah, an inspiration! And now I remember, your 'fabric art' is Asian, isn't it? At least, that's how it was described in the newspaper story that got passed around the class."

"It is now. For many years I was reluctant to use images and techniques of a country this country wanted to forget. And I was profoundly unskilled in their fine methods. So, I took up Ozark folk art, the authentic homegrown style which the Hillbilly Shed generally bastardizes."

"From high-end toilets—pun intended—to the Butt Dump."

She laughed. "As I said, at times I find genuinely fine wall hangings and floor mats at the Hillbilly Shed. But, anyway, in the last ten years or so, after a lot of concentrated study, I began to produce works that Nguyet might have been proud to see."

"You're making me regret I never looked seriously at Vietnamese art. We were over there to preserve their way of life, but I took no time to learn about their traditions."

"Your job was to relay to the folks back home that their sons and husbands and friends were protecting them from Communism. At least that's what we thought at the time. And I know you did it well."

"I'm almost afraid to ask, but what happened to . . . your teacher?"

"She just disappeared. I never found out. I even requested the help of my colleagues, but . . . nothing."

Curtis was thoughtful. "Now Americans, including Vietnamese War vets like ourselves, travel to Vietnam and have a wonderful time. I've never been myself, but they report that they love the food, the architecture, the music. Well, they did until a world-wide pandemic put a stop to that kind of travel."

"Yes, tourism was the way for that poor, war-ravaged country to survive. Capitalism and commerce are roads to prosperity, but there is always a price. Just as the Shed brings down the quality of rural folk art, so the tourist industry there has muddied their culture."

"We were like tobacco to that country, a drug that satisfied for a time, but was fatal in the end."

She studied the landscape. "And here's another thing. We're in a period of isolationism now, which is being intensified by Covid-19. We are cutting ourselves off from cultural traditions that might improve our way of life."

"Traditions that are not about profit and loss. Goods are generally traded, right, through a barter system, not sold? They're not commodities."

"Right. It's why I'm interested in folk art in many countries. Hmm. Perhaps this pandemic is a good time, after all, to take stock of what matters. If we're to do more than just survive the coronavirus—that is, learn about ourselves and our past to make a better future—we need to value . . . ," she pulled her purchase out of her purse and laughed, "the Butt Dump and not the tobacco!"

Michael Lund

Our Island Home

He's been all over this place: from the backward communities in
the Northern Territory, where discrimination is still prevalent —
to the home of corrupted politics in our nation's capital, he's
experienced the riches and beauty, he's experienced the racism,
ugliness and greed: he belongs to Australia, originally from a
rural town in India, but he is proud to call this home with his
family even though there are some that will try to deny him.
He drove me home in his Holden Captiva, I gave him five stars
for his professionalism, engaging conversations and safety on
the road. He's more *Aussie* than those that chant *True Blue*.
He cares more about the economy than the parasitises in
parliament. We say our farewells, but maybe we'll meet again
in the future. I'm happy to call him a brother and welcome
him to our land of First Nations and diverse multi-cultures.

Jayden Martin

Waiting for the snow
After Cavafy's 'Waiting for the Barbarians'

Like the barbarians

the snow is coming

yet so unlike.

Yes, it is forecast

over and over

false rumour flying

the flakes criss-crossing

never settling.

But there's no panic

no swirling exodus

no freezing dread.

Only the still longing

for the soft white

the stretched light

the invasion of peace.

Penny McCarthy

The Prize Counter Anomaly

the world was built
for dollhouses and toolboxes
gifted to the binaries
and i am an anomaly
built for blurring lines.

i'm reminded
that my reality
is that of a prize counter
at an arcade of arcane proportion —
children turn in tokens
for a slew of insurmountable questions,
musings, any close-minded thoughts
that flow with no filter,
yet they still receive a prize
for approaching the counter.

i'm picked apart
and traded for a plastic frog
that jumps with a push to its back,
a yo-yo destined to be tangled,
five minutes of satisfaction
that no one really needed,

but the convenience of
turning in tokens
with no repercussions
makes me the sole representative
of the Prize Counter Anomaly,
a line-blurring, binary-botching
token of easy access.

Alfie Ormsbee

What My Dear Has Come To

What do you say when your husband lies so
softly still on a strange stretcher?
Four men heft him out our front door
with screen cinched open. "See you
later?" passes through my mind.

I stand by his elevated bed soon enough.
Light zig-zags on a screen — pictures of
my lover's heart. A nurse inserts needle
in his vein's blue thread. I look from above
and see his scalp's bare circle has expanded.

What say we after the doctor slips off —
that luxuriantly-haired man. My hubbie quips,
"Used to be doctors were older."
What we can't say, *How soon
the limitless days to do this or that
shrink. Our bodies shrivel.*
What comes? Pill cases and CVS trips,
rigid routines, MD or PT appointments,
failing sight and DMV decisions.

The past shoves into mind — my dad
dodders on his cane, beet neck wrinkled like
his leather shammy. Though he yielded steering
wheel, he still rode me. *Not here. Turn there.*
Craning at labels in the grocery, I near his side,
Don't rush me! he whines.

I stand by my man, reclining in quiet.
My queries foment. Unknowing
what's beyond the curve ahead,
clouds of dust or blossoms.

Carol Park

Bird in the Rain

The bird is tall.
It stands upright
on dancer's legs.

A neat curve
of fawn breast
is speckled
to perfection
with chocolate brown.

This bird has strength
at its core.
There is tension
in the angle
of its neck
below quick eyes.

It knows when
to hold the pause,
and when to haul

a silken worm,
enchanted,
from the soft, wet soil.

Janet Philo

Rooted in The North-South Road

It began with desire,
then the wait,
before the hope
of you took root.

That day,
you became
a someone,
deep inside, as
I vomited into the verge.

The limestone horse saw it all.
The white horse on the hill
pretends radiance,
but when the sun goes down,
he's nothing.

Sunset warms
the sandstone squares
of the roadside church,
peach cheeks them,
pomegranate pinks them,
honey suckles them,
as sunlight paints me
home.

Sandstone catches light
and throws it
at the greying horse,
shines him white again
and shows me
my road home,
and back,
and home
and back again,
until I do not know
which way is home,
and which is back,

and only know
that something
has begun.

Janet Philo

Blue-eyed Boy

It's not their colour, the drowse of the lids
     more
          a shadow moving under the surface

the arching of an eyebrow
          a lure landing like a kiss on still water

a gaze caught in your gut
          drawing you closer and closer
till you lie gasping
          in the dust
             and dirt of his broken life.

Jenna Plewes

Still life with Peaches

Who bruised you,
left those marks on your velvety skin?

Did his paint-spattered fingers squeeze
to test your ripeness;

did he breathe in the scent of musk
before he placed you — so — beside the other,

turned you so the light stroked your body,
slid into that cunning pink cleft?

And when he was done, did he sink his teeth
through the downy surface into moist flesh, slide

his tongue round the pitted stone, extricate
your heart and leave it on a messy plate?

Jenna Plewes

Deucalion

In the flood of words and images
are blood-red arterial folds like wine,
like deepest Saturn; Venusian mists

revealing vast cemeteries of the enlightened,
Niagaras of ecstasy, great breaches
in the encrusted sea-walls.

My beginnings were invaginated,
within labia of green and grey.
The suffering stars embank and gaze,

explosant-fixé, like Cornelia Parker's
exploding shed emblazoned in the yellow haze.
Great wings lap my waves in the morning light,

ultra-violet, ultra-rhapsodic,
enwrapt, wrapped in the vision,
enucleated, the mind's eye riven,

driven, a place of lighter learning
(whatever that might be), the sun burning;
there is no respite from being flayed.

Gulls' wings, a ragged sacerdotalism,
the morbid oceanic terror of liturgy
orbiting a chaotic centre, whirlpools

of desire, endless elasticities of trajectory,
distillation of colour preparations,
marine palettes of the luminous.

In me word becomes colour, colour becomes
word, word becomes (encloses) the void —
a-void the word, the transparent metal petal.

Not all seas are ethereal, some are sticky
with pith and resin, the result of ceaseless
Seahorses' hooves ripping at the fabric.

Are there words on the swaying curtains,
on the reefs' ruches, their velvet settees?
I am a blue screen to play the universe,

a silent scream, or sometimes something worse.
Solace of centuries and curer of old wounds,
what aphrodisiac heartsease could describe

this lust for life; I pause to think of ghosts
who only care for misled sounds. On my surface
the witch-wind is blowing from nowhere.

David Punter

Space Poem

I want
    to feel space
        in this poem

I want
    to be free
        of the constraints
of rhyme and rhythm

I want
    there to be space
        for marauding ghosts

flapping their sepia wings
    in darkness

and also room for
    my grandmother
        in her sagging

maroon dress covering
    the wounds
        of two cancers

I want
    a dam to burst
        and a discreet flood

of images to pour
    pale-opalescent
        tears over the feet

of idols
    while I
        lounge indolently

pointing at language
    doing my bidding
        while knowing

in the silent span
    that I am her victim too
        her supplicant

Grandma's English
    was halting
        inflected with Welsh
especially on a Wednesday

(half-day at school)
    when she would feed me
        spotted dick

and I once cut my finger
    to the bone
        picking gooseberries

(gooseberries — is there space
    to wonder
        why 'gooseberries'?)

birds can't touch then,
    she said,
        there's no space

between the prickles —
    the same prickles
        you feel at your shoulder

when the ghosts come
    jostling for space
        hopeful of attention
a renegade band of dear ones

and the space
    will never run out
        on me, on us

the merest glimpse
   of a maroon dress
      and the horrors

it might conceal
   makes me yearn
      for space

between words, among
   prickles, thorns,
      where birds

can neither land nor peck
   nor eat their bushel
      while hiding

their light from the light
   which is the light
      of space
where the ghosts all
   have room for their habitation.

David Punter

Counting Down the Days

i.
Won't you miss the status?
I think of high-heeled, toe-pinching shoes,
boring meetings, men stealing my words,
smart dresses and suits with no personality,
the smell of dry-cleaning fluid.
No, I bloody won't.

I bet you'll want to work,
you'll miss the routine, the people.
I think of people I've disciplined,
back stabbers in the hierarchy.
Early mornings, late nights, endless traffic.
Time racing, blurs of emails, deadlines
and always

more and more to do. I nod, scream
NO, in my head. *You'll be missed.*
I smile my thanks, know my job
will go. I'll soon be forgotten.
I start deleting files, forward
a few useful reports, wave goodbye
to PowerPoint presentations,
without a backward glance.

ii.
Days hold   their   breath
they have   no punctuation   yet
but pause   stutter   stop
start   a dance   to   my rhythm
shut   out   years   of   driving   beat

I   daydream   in sun   take meals out   shop
with my daughter   until   we   drop
swim   read   visit forgotten   people
holiday   with no   sad goodbye
clock   each   dandelion   mouse   cuckoo
fuck   with abandon   fight   laugh with eyes

83

iii.

Years short-circuit   stop   need to hold   on
grip fear   don't let it   in   wait
known world   waits   hangs
like droplets   breath in fog
filters   through   masks

Jenny Robb

beyond the boardwalk

they were so proud of the new boardwalk
lit up by garlands and stands of lightbulbs
with railings and trashcans and benches
built over the exquisite silver sands
studded with shells and starfish
before the ocean's shifting tideline

but they wouldn't come with us
after dark, none of the men
wanted to walk with us on the boards
in the tropical sea-filled night
where beyond the electric illumination
the moon breathed on the sea
and the sea breathed at the moon

so we three girls gathered our skirts
and set out along the illuminated way
where we met no bodies or villains
no druggies or *flaneurs* no lechers
no leering fools no-one at all

but lovers down on the moonlit sands
were kissing the skin of the dark
caressing the heaving sea
licking the salt of the sea
letting the sea lick their feet
wetting their hands with the sea
giving themselves to the sea
letting the ocean enter them

all along the coast they were
drowning in the midnight sea

Gillie Robic

I am clad in exhaustion

All I want is to sleep
– no –
all I want is to look at the ocean
– no –
all I want is to look at the sky
where I was flying away.

The sea is full of stars
streaming into the breakers,
sparking out on the sand.

Wash and glitter overwhelm
the acoustic darkness.
Stars flicker round my feet,
I wade into the sky.

Gillie Robic

Rewinding Time

She taught me how to wind her clock,
open its smooth chocolate walnut door
and with my shaking hands pause
the tick-tock of pendulous infinity,
before turning the ornate wrought
iron key clockwise, until resistance
said enough. I'd reintroduce the
weight to its repetitive dance and
close the door on the week ahead.
When finished, my Nan would smile
across her clean, creased face that shone
like polished leather, huge spectacle lenses
like bay windows of a house
that saw everything without
a hint of any curtain twitch.
Mum's voice, long distance in my first
term away a surprise, her words
fall rhythmically, like Nan's clock.
Nan   cross   road   hit   car   drunk.
Intoxicated hands that had ceased
Nan's movement with no regard
for restarting a gentle sway, back
and forth from house to corner shop.

Stephen Roe

Jynxed

Jynx the sorceress made Zeus fall for Io. Hera his wife's revenge was to turn Jynx into a wryneck bird whose head-twists, hisses and contortions suggested magical properties. In Ancient Greece wrynecks were tied to wheel-like charms (Iynxes) and set spinning to foretell the future.

1

Through ghosts of fields
under paved estates
a heifer thunders where orchards were,
comes to a pawing halt in the dark —
the moon-glow of its hide echoes
the lantern-sway of apple blossom.
Io once had a moon to herself
but now she snorts and drools.
Zeus crashes through branches in search of her.

Trapped inside a wryneck
the sorceress Jynx,
hissing from a hole in the tree,
writhes her head like a temple dancer —
no chance of further answer.
A Jaguar bellows down the drive.
This is Hera's revenge on Zeus

2

Snake-bird calling
on my phone that wakes —
conjure for me upon this screen
a text that she will have me back
and all these scattered fragments turn
not-real into what's real.

3

My wife's phone is full of dark matter these days
pendulum-weights, plunge-drops,
her Sim-card conceals chasms
where snakeskins slither —
I once caught a serpent looking at me
as she sipped coffee,
she tongue-flicked and smiled at her screen
spinning its vibrations right there.

If I thought she did not love me
no roof could house my folly.

I scroll through our wedding photos
but she has vacated the room —
I hear the ping of a thousand creatures
delighting her
across the lounge, up the staircase,
on the divans of our executive home.

My socked feet crossing the bedroom carpet
trying not to stalk her
leave hoof-prints at body-heat.

4
But what about Io months ago?
That doe-eyed one returned my look and we trafficked in bluebells,
                    dealt musk, sniffed wild garlic on our fingers.

5
Why is her wedding dress buried in the wardrobe?
Why shove these wedding shoes under the floorboards?
Where are the deeds of our house in their strongbox?
Catch yourself smelling the scent of her bathrobe,
stealing her phone like a safe locked and loaded,
a war-chest, a briefcase of missile codes.

When did my lies carve such shape-shifting folly
plumbing the shallows, swerving the depths?
When did the heart mistake satin for spandex
spangled with debts? Each wave and the next
make a set. Send a text. Her boss's Jag scrunches
the drive, then they kiss. In deep. I watch near to death.

6
No cuckoo on our new estate,
only collared doves that mock the Spring.
A cuckold in shorts, I wheel out the rubbish
turn on the oven, warm up each plate,
spin and spin my wedding ring
as abysses starts to sing
in the seas of the dishwasher.

Flee the house to the orchard end
searching for wryneck, the cuckoo's mate,
ignore the kids and our neighbour waving —
I spin around on a wheel-like charm:
Jynx has trapped me and tied me fast.
Hera, my wife, turns her back when I return.
Truth or dare in human form? her silence says.

7
Desire's electric friction
just generates fiction.
Jynx, begetter of this
is there something in your very nest
makes these serpent-eggs that rock and tap
to crack the human heart?

Graeme Ryan

Song

It is the hem of a song in a fold of the wind,
in a pocket of air, before the day zips up again, tight-lipped —

a song like the waft of steak
down summer alleyways from a heat-wave kitchen,
the juice of a song melting somewhere into nowhere,
the sweetest sex of saxophone from an open
apartment window before the engines of artics
blast-furnace the street with blue diesel
and sirens burrow down rush hour to the cells and the wards —

it is the first bars of *Say A Little Prayer For Me*
in a Detroit diner, dissolving in the stained sugar bowl
and the smell of cheap coffee and grits —
just a taste of the voice of Aretha
in the intervals between notes on car-horns
segued to plate-scrape and nicotine-clatter of cutlery —

it is the call of the muezzin
the gull-cry which hits
the chord in A minor of the anchorite
it is bells through shoals of leaves spinning the wind
into threads of gold for the Abbess at evensong —

micro-tones of the Bulgarian choir, the Indian temple singer,
there are robes this song is wearing and this is how the heart thinks —

Pastora Pavon, Lorca's flamenco *duende*
slugging a glass of fire-water brandy in a Cadiz tavern:
the flame that burns in her throat lights a torch
through the dark caverns of Franco and the smoke of Guernica —

Amazing Grace as the protestors head across the bridge
into the water cannon and gunshots —
it is the song which undoes us at Columbine
in Florida, in Sandy Hook, at the funerals of children,
pulling wires through us, performing open-heart surgery —

this song works deep tissue
in the cells, it shakes us again and again
grabbing our breath

we are crying, we don't know why
we are just wavelengths in ocean

Graeme Ryan

You're feeling guilty. You shouldn't feel guilty. Nothing happened. He took you to a tapas bar for lunch. You shared plates of garlic prawns, hot pimentos and rich cheeses. You drank sangria as if it was lemonade. He showed you photos of his house in Esher with its tennis courts and indoor pool. You showed him photos of your kids: the terrible twins Zak and Max; Lara, thirteen yesterday. A beauty like her Mum he said. You don't tell him how she kept you awake half the night, celebrating with her mates, creating havoc, refusing to turn her music down. He doesn't have children, just two golden retrievers. Afterwards you both took a stroll around the City, giggling at office gossip. He asked if you would like to see the new state of the art building, gesturing towards a tangle of concrete and glass scraping the sky. Not a good idea, you said. He brushed a crumb from your face, his sharp eyes locking with yours. You considered telling him your greatest secret but he suddenly remembered he had a meeting in ten minutes. A peck on the cheek and you caught a bus back to St Pancras, imagining how your life might have been.

A peck on the cheek. That was all.

You have an hour to kill before your train so you amble through Coal Drops Yard entranced by the eclectic mix of shops and stalls. You try on a snazzy red dress which is way above your price range, parade in front of the mirror as though you are hosting a party at his Esher mansion. You buy it without feeling in the slightest bit guilty. You browse an arts and crafts market, buy a woven bracelet for Lara, some chocolate for Steve and the twins. Then you sit on the steps overlooking Regents Canal sipping a latte. The area is throbbing with the pulse of redevelopment. Thirteen years since you lived and worked in London. But everything has changed.

An incoming call: Steve.

"I thought you'd be home by now."

"You told me not rush back."

"Ok, ok, just the place is a tip, Lara's mates are still here, the twins are driving me round the twist."

"Take them to the beach."

"But what about Lara?"

"Lara can take care of herself. And her guests. Look I'm at the station now. Almost."

"How did the appointment go?"

"The appointment? Oh, I'll er tell you about it when I get back."

"Christ now what's she done. Lara! Must go."

Ten minutes until your train departs. You start to make your way through the throngs of commuters towards the station, try not to look in any more shop windows, try to come up with a plausible excuse for missing your appointment. That's when you see it. Just before the station entrance a pillar on the pavement displays various information leaflets. Staring down from a wanted poster is your photo. Of course it can't be you, yet the resemblance is uncanny. Beneath the photo you can make out the words 'dangerous' and 'should not be approached.' Light rain has begun to fall blurring your vision. You want to get a closer look but supposing someone notices the resemblance? You glance behind you at the crowds rushing past, putting up hoods or umbrellas, fingering their phones. You start to breathe again and quicken your pace towards the station, all sound drowned by the echoing percussion of your heartbeat.

The five twenty-five to Margate is delayed. You find the ladies room, tidy yourself. You tweak your hair, spray a mist of Chanel around your face, try to keep your hand steady as you apply lipstick. You notice a red wine stain on your blouse. How will you explain it? You rub and scrub until your blouse is drenched but it won't come out. You remember the dress you just bought. Easier to explain a new dress than a wine stain. You go into one of the cubicles and change. When you come out you see it. Above the sign saying 'now wash your hands.' The photo. Unmistakably you. You remember Steve taking it in Ibiza when you had sunburn. Not a flattering photo, your scowling face is swollen and red. The caption beneath it reads:
WANTED FOR MURDER. THIS PERSON SHOULD NOT BE APPROACHED UNDER ANY CIRCUMSTANCES BUT CALL_

A woman enters the facility with a noisy toddler. You push past into the main concourse. You are terrified of missing your train but you daren't risk being wrongly mistaken for this criminal. Your phone is ringing; Steve's ringtone. You ignore the call. The final whistle blasts for the delayed service to Margate. Hiding your face with your scarf you join the stampede for the train. No seats so you stand crushed against damp coats, breathing aromas of sweat and stale aftershave. You, a killer. Kitty Wolf. Should not be approached. You half smile at the absurdity of it. You wonder if someone in the office knows about you and Lance. Someone who seeks revenge. The notorious Lance. How many personal assistants has he had affairs with since you left, you wonder? How many other broken hearts?

But supposing there had been a murder? Had something happened to Lance? The wine stain on your blouse. What if it's not wine, but *blood*.

The train stops at Stratford International; passengers spill out and you make for a seat. You hear a text come in: *So lovely to see you again, Kitty. L. xx*

He's alive! There has been no murder. The photo wasn't you after all. You grin at the city-suited man sitting next to you who glares back.

You gaze out of the window seeing and not seeing row after row of grey houses, smoky industrial estates, traffic thronged roads. Your eyes are slowly closing. You find yourself naked in a sea of towering waves, playing hide-and-seek with Lance. A crowd has gathered on the beach, watching. Among them you spot Steve, Zak and Max and Lara. You wonder if they suspect Lance is Lara's father. You want to hide but there's nowhere. No-where to hide apart from the ocean roaring behind you.

A sharp jolt wakes you. The train has stopped in the middle of a rain-sodden field. A miserable voice through a public address system apologises for the delay, apparently due to a signalling problem. The man next to you shakes and folds his newspaper.

He turns to you, "and they call this high speed," he grumbles.

You nod sympathetically. The train spurts, screeches then crawls forward a mile or two before pausing again. Grassy banks tower either side of the carriages, strewn with litter, plastic bags cling to bushes like collapsed lungs. A murmuration of starlings swoop down from the sky and sit chatting on the parapet of a graffiti-covered bridge. The train edges forward. You stare at the graffiti in disbelief. Bubble writing blazes in colours of the rainbow, each letter outlined in red, dripping like blood, spelling out the words: 'KITTY WOLF IS THE DEVIL.' 'KITTY WOLF MUST DIE.'

This is your guilt. Of course it's your guilt. Not you, just your guilt. If only you had kept your appointment you could have talked about it. But recently things had seemed better. You were coping. You needed a break, that's all. A day out on your own. Away from the house and the kids.

The man next to you is constantly fidgeting with the pages of his newspaper to demonstrate his frustration. Other passengers are napping or texting, music and muffled conversations leaking from their phones. You have the strangest feeling that you are being watched by someone. You've no idea who or where.

The train starts up again, rattling through a tunnel. You ought to text Steve, he'll be going berserk. But you need to work out what to say. And anyway there's no signal on your phone. You glance at the man's newspaper as he turns a page and catch the headline: *Birthday Party Massacre: mother who murdered still on the run.* There is a grainy photo of Steve and the kids taken several years ago beside a photo of you, nurturing an evil twisted smirk.

You make it to the lavatory just in time to throw up. You bolt the door and sit on the toilet bowl until your head stops spinning, trying to think rationally. What to do. What to do. You hate yourself for leaving Steve on his own to cope. For making up lies. For meeting an old lover. For leaving Lara and her friends, even though she had insisted you went.

You want to hug them all, spend the night in Steve's arms the way you once did.

The sour smelling cubicle is unbearably claustrophobic but you are terrified to leave. Is this how it will feel, you wonder, shut up in a tiny prison cell for life? The door rattles from time to time as passengers try the handle. Crackly announcements broadcast names of commuter towns then seaside destinations: Sittingbourne, Faversham, Herne Bay, Birchington-on-Sea. This is a loop line. After Margate, the train will carry on to Dover then back to St Pancras. It occurs to you that if you stay in here, you could go round and round forever. Round and round and round. Never be found.

A fuzzy announcement comes through the speaker: "We will shortly be arriving at Margate. Passengers should check they have all their belongings before alighting from the train."

You have to face up to the truth, whatever that truth is. You know you have nothing to hide. You open the door, slowly sidle back to your carriage. The city-suited man's seat is empty but he has left his newspaper behind, carefully folded. And there, on your seat is your phone. Fingers trembling you snatch it up to make the dreaded call.

The screen displays a message from Lara: Hate Kayley mum, she's not my friend any more. When are you home?

Your squeal of joy rips through the carriage. You are wanted. Wanted by your family. They are alive.

You pick up the newspaper from the man's seat and flick through every page. No mention of you. No picture of Steve and the kids. Nothing but news and ads.

❊

Margate. The overpowering smell of seaweed as you come out of the station. The mocking cries of gulls. Above the horizon streaks of crimson float in an inky sky, the last lingering remnants of sunset. You walk along the front past boarded-up amusement arcades, gaudy graffiti proclaiming: 'Jaz and Kevin forever,' 'Chris loves Sam.' A sharp wind sends a flurry of litter whirling around you. A 'wanted' leaflet falls at your feet. You pick it up, your heart banging, waves of sickness washing over you. But the photo is of some seasoned criminal, a middle-aged man with a crazed stare. You toss it away and turn off towards the old town with its retro shops, quirky cafes and galleries. You remember why you and Steve fell in love with the area. Shoreditch-on-Sea they call it. You both worked so hard to make things work, at first.

Your phone pings. A text: *Hope you got home safely. Lets meet again soon* X

Your heart is racing. So temping to arrange another date. A lunch or a weekend in a hotel. But you know it would be madness. You reply: *Sorry. Today was a mistake. My family need me.*

You feel sad, but strong. You will never see Lance again. He will never know he has a daughter. But then you were never completely sure.

A boozy smell hits you as you let yourself into the house. You move discarded take-away containers, crisp packets and cans out of your way.

"Anyone in?"

The living room door opens, Steve appears rubbing bloodshot eyes from a nap.

"Ah, at last. Enjoyed yourself?"

The twins tumble out of the kitchen, ketchup smeared faces, too busy pretending to shoot each other to notice you.

"Bang, bang you're dead."

"Bang, bang, so are you."

Lara appears on the staircase wearing an assortment of your clothes and make-up, her mates in tow.

"Go away Mum. We're fine."

"You messaged me to hurry up."

"I've made up with Kayley. Can she stay tonight, too?"

"No, Lara. Your party is over now."

You take off your coat, go into the living room, flop on to the sofa.

"Someone want to put the kettle on?" you ask, kicking off your shoes.

Steve notices the red dress.

"What on earth are you wearing?"

"Like it? I thought we could treat ourselves to a night out if we can find a sitter."

"And I suppose I'm paying for it. The same as I paid for this ridiculously expensive therapy session you didn't turn up for."

"How do you know?"

"I called to query the amount. They said you'd cancelled."

"I don't need therapy Steve, just…"

"Babe, it's been a pig of a day. You made me take time off so you could go gallivanting around London, telling me nothing but a pack of lies. Hey what's all this?"

He empties your bag. The gifts you bought and your soiled blouse tumble on to the floor.

"Explain."

You can't explain. The house is caving in on you. You reach to pick up your things but Steve grabs the neck of your dress. As you pull away it rips down the front. Something snaps in your brain. Hateful words tumble out of your mouth like weapons. You confess to infidelities, affairs that you have no recollection of, anything to wound him. The twins are jumping up and down with the frenzy of an audience at a boxing match.

Lara shouts at you both to shut up in front of her mates. Steve wallops her backside. You scream at him to leave Lara alone.

"She's not even your child!" you hear yourself say.

In the electric silence that follows, you wonder why you said it. You wonder if you can unsay it. But before you attempt to explain, Steve lunges at you, his punch misses your face but lands on your breastbone.

The humiliation is worse than the pain. Wordlessly you leave the room. You go into the kitchen, put the kettle on, place a teabag in a mug.

Something deep inside you is shifting, changing. Someone is telling you what to do. It's her. The other you. The one who occupies your body and your mind. The other you knows there is a way out of this mess. The other you takes a swig of gin from the bottle you keep at the back of the odds-and-sods drawer, then pulls a knife down from the rack. The carving knife. You stare at the distorted reflection on the shiny blade, bruised flesh bursting out of the torn red dress, mouth contorting into an evil twisted smirk.

Yvonne Sampson

Ode to Gravitas

Gravity takes hold of me,
Tummy sags below breasts flat like pancakes on the grill.

Knees scream out in pain
Now, a tingling chorus burns with song beneath my toes

I tell myself each pain means I'm still alive.
I squish my nose up and with wide eyes keep myself from crying out loud.

Where do those tears go?
The ones I push back and down.

Perhaps Tummy is a well of tears
And not the sugar I eat.

I tell myself it's zaftig, I'm a Renoir woman, round and full,
Blossoming pink like a bud of Spring Venus.

Or tummy roundness as beautiful as the pregnant mother,
Growing a baby inside her.

Inside of me resides a child, I say.
A child who will be born to me.

A child who has always been my guide
Pulling strings so that my imagination expands.

And so, I like to think of roundness as a gift from God,
Maybe even my true self whom I've been nurturing all these seventy-six years.

Sometimes harshly with the push and pull
Sometimes with a kick in the pants, "Get going," I say.

Sometimes with a nudge, "Go at your own pace."
Sometimes with a stillness.

I breathe, hear the birds, feel the wind on my face, touch
The softness of the hairs on my cheeks, downy like a baby's.

I hear my eighteen-year-old granddaughter say, "Granny, I love to touch
Your face. It's so soft and smooth. I missed that the most in quarantine."

Aw! Her long fingers brush the down the way she pats Charlie, her cat, so
That the fur goes in the same direction.

Fur going in the same direction
I can meet my feline nature as an independent, lovely old cat, rooted to the earth,

Waiting in the sunlight stroked by Breeze, warmed by Sun, serenaded by Birdsong,
Holding my pregnant belly in my hand to be born once again.

Barbara Sapienza

Tulips for a new house

I wake spinning like a compass seeking north,
cold in a space of white walls
too far away, unpadded by books,
where the windows are in the wrong place.

We've swapped sirens and bumper parking,
a scrap of green strewn with kebab wrappings
for a lawn, a magnolia, a pond of frogs,
an up-and-over garage, a gate.

We are silent about the sadness of leaving
our Egyptian newsagent with his campaign
against porn, Gino's lemon sorbet, bagels
eaten warm in alleys late at night.

Here the new green is blinding
and the welcome tulips from my sister
hang open, red and rude,
glossy with the threat of Spring.

Helen Scadding

White Island

I join you on your island twice a month.
I am punctual, mooring carefully, so that I can leave promptly.

I find you hunkering down among the armchairs
washed up in a clearing of white space.

The walnut bureau looms above a scattering of flotsam
finger-worn fish knives, napkin rings, forgotten glasses.

Today it is tropical, the steam rising from radiators
spread with sheets, pyjamas and pants.

In the distance the falling notes of a flute,
and the purr of machines settling in for the night.

You have stopped going to the edges to look out.
You move slowly, staring down, as though searching for a coin

lost in this familiar place where the rooms fall in
upon themselves and all around is the swell of other lives.

Helen Scadding

Still Lives

The fallen-down pigeon is as big as her doll.
The wind blows its feathers
like Mummy blows her pasta when it is too hot.
Strange how it is asleep with its eyes open wide.
Perhaps it is looking for its mummy and daddy.
She is sure that they won't be long.

Dad has told him all about death.
How if he was squashed by a car
he wouldn't see anybody ever again. Never.
Nothing has squashed this frog though. The opposite.
Its stomach is inflated tight, like a beach ball.
He was the first in class to shoot up his hand
when Miss had wanted a better word for blown up!
Look. Tiny flies are sliding like skaters across its eyes.
Dad had told him everything stops when you are dead,
not that he could imagine himself ever stopping.

Tomorrow his surgeon with pickpocket's fingers
will deftly slice him open to have a little peek inside,
a delve around. A look-see. Nothing to get too alarmed about.
After all the stats were all in his favour. Absolutely.
So why does he lay awake, waiting to be unwrapped,
worrying what this present to himself could be?

She is doing remarkably well, for her age.
Everyone tells her that: doctors, visitors, chaplains.
This is just background noise, bursts of static,
a distraction from her listening out.
Instead she stares out at a space
for beyond the ward, straining, straining
to catch the first glimpse of the gatecrasher,
that uninvited guest who spoils everyone's party.

Dave Smith

Viking, North Utsire

She is the first to arrive because she always is.
He will arrive ten minutes later,
as punctual as the shipping forecast.

Checking her face in the driving mirror:
non-committal, guarded, ageing,
her desperation — or is it boredom? —
lies buried deep, weighted down.
An inconvenient corpse.

By now the sex is as routine as door to door inquiries
and as predictable as the tides.

She pulls hard on her cigarette
— as luck would have it his wife smokes too! —
and forces herself to concentrate on the ways
the breeze moves through the branches.
Mindfulness. Her therapist's trick.

Next, pigtailed again, she chews pink bubble gum
which will lose its flavour just as he draws up.

Later he will ask her
"Why didn't we meet ten years ago?" adding
"I only stay for the kids, you know that."
The Tyne, Dogger, Fisher of infidelity.

Tonight though the general synopsis seems set fair,
no attention all shipping, no warning of gales.
Yet, as he speaks, she finds herself
responding to the rise and fall of his voice
much as a trawler rides the swell in Viking, North Utsire,
not listening to the words, realising that promises
are so much more reassuring than the truth
provided that you do not believe in them.

Dave Smith

is a cubby hole full of books, one book a bit longer than the rest, in the bottom corner, Len Hutton's autobiography.

As soon as I open it, the musk of a hastily milked byre hits me, I can feel the barley horns pricking my fingers from getting the last stooks in so we could to Scarborough the next day.

Yorkshire were playing Kent and the "Man" was on 46 NOT OUT on his way to another hundred.

Mother fussing, "have you got your mac, it could be doing anything over there", as I squirmed clutching my biscuit tin, with its purple stained jam sandwiches, a scone, a sausage roll and a couple of apples from the orchard.

Dad is filling the radiator on the old Austin, plenty of hills between us and the ground.

Hutton got his hundred just before tea with a lofted drive over mid on. The man next me explained that it was the first shot that had left the carpet. Apparently he came from the next village to Pudsey where Hutton was born, had known him all his life.

At the interval coming out of the gents Hutton was standing just yards from me, in his whites, cap askew, Yorkshire cap of course, drinking a cup of tea. I suppose he must drink cups of tea like everybody else, but it was a bit of a shock.

Other thing he only had one pad on, when this was discussed with Fatty, Enoch and Gaffer at home, Gaffer who knew about these things said

"There must be a reason for him doing that, best not pry, there will definitely be a reason" - well maybe, but I'm still waiting.

They said I fell asleep on the way back, clutching my heavily marked score card, and a stick of rock for Ted our farm lad who had milked, fothered up that evening.

Deep in my trousers was the tea-spoon with Scarborough Castle on the top. It would go in the little glass fronted cupboard alongside the one from Llandudno, Blackpool, Whitby and the special Edinburgh one from their honeymoon.

The book gets a bit heavy now, the words start to blur, so I slip it back into to its place, I usually put him with someone he can talk to; he spent a bit of time with Ted Hughes but somehow I thought there would a lot of West Yorkshire silences.

Seamus Heaney is there now, looking a bit warm in his thick, green tweed three-piece suit, but I think they'll get on, Seamus being Irish and all.

David Smith

Meteors and Vampires

flew low and fast

into my childhood

I counted the seconds

between sight and sound

lightening and thunder

safe home after Korea, Malaya

they played hide and seek

in hills and valleys

tag with their echoes

skimmed trees frightened sheep

left me

in the trance

of their vapour

"I want to do that"

David Smith

Lizzy Borden

Lizzy holds a sign
with Ladies of the Christian Temperance Unit
protesting Dr Couney's wet nurses drinking stout
It's like giving infants a bottle of beer!
It's an abortion of common sense

The sky is forbidding at Coney Island
as she strolls the boardwalk
Side shows of The Headless Woman and The Human Worm
sets her brain whirling
she pulls at her hair
takes a swig from her flask
wanders in a daze
recalls tweezing eyeballs of Fall River rats
splitting them in two
dangling grey bodies by their tails
      snipping off each leg
           snip snap snip
      always saving the throat 'til last
      listening for the engine of their last breath

    I'm just not cut out to be a mother

Alone on the beach she sings
when I needed water the earth was dry
crushed heads with grey sludgy veins wash onto shore
axe blades deep in their skulls
a family portrait she cannot erase
she begins to strip off
buries her dress in the sand

Kathleen Strafford

Molly Brown
To call a ship unsinkable is flying in the face of God

12:00 midnight
The White Star lights up like Coney Island flashing 3 dots 3 dashes 3 dots

2:00 am
A trio play their immortal requiem
boilers explode clean through the stern
       waves call out names for the cortege
         throats curve against cabin doors with faces
        desperate to escape their heads
           free-fall splashing
               into the blue oubliette.

Its storm rail points straight to dead stars glowing
with a sense of duty
Molly orders the boatswain to rescue
        the drenched & shivering
        on coffin plates.

3:00am
Abandoned even by the moon   cold darkness splashes
oars brushing away the brined   salted
              & pickled in mid-ocean.
Crew with whistles frozen to their lips
             baptised mothers still caressing their silent angels.

9:00 am
Confused, dazed by the sun's glare
Molly stays behind carrying an infant.
       Dr Couney and his nurse
         ambulance the injured to hospitals
           offer to take the orphan into their care.

80 years later
Amongst broken plates   butterfly comb left on a dresser
the piano continues its underwater echo of a mermaid's waltz
Spectacles float magnifying the piano's warped teeth
                              playing notes now only found in bottles.
                                   Shoes stopped mid dance-step wait
                                        for the next chord.

Kathleen Strafford

Migration
after Ellie Harrison

They remember
the taste of the river
the smell of gravel
as familiar as instinct
that pulls them
through cold heavy seas
feel an old acquaintance
with sunlit pools
in salt free water
buffering against autumn
the narrows of gorges
challenges of cataracts
to the place of spawning
changed from grey to red
in the reed bed of birth
resting place
homecoming.

Kate Swann

Murmuration

Liquid stars weave a bone pale sky
dancers in the evening light
swaying   shifting
in balletic ripples
drifting in unison
to the whirr of wings
whose movement is barely
visible to the awestruck crowd
a seventh sense calls the moment when
you gather from all four corners
darken the shimmering sky
how do you know which
way to go   where to turn
when to leave for your
homebound journey

Kate Swann

I Cannot Tell

The forest calls me from the beach. My tar-caked legs walk me under the trees.

A man sits on a boulder in the dimmed light of the forest.

He eats an overstuffed sandwich. He stuffs one giant bite after another down his gullet. Again, and again, and again.

"I'm so hungry," I yell.

"As am I," he responds.

Soon, I cannot tell if the moon is so bright or the sun is so dim. I cannot tell. I cannot tell.

The sky is mesmerizing.

Rain pours down.

"Just my luck," I say unmoved.

"Just *our* luck," the sandwich man says, undeterred from eating. "On what slender threads do life and fortune hang."

"That sounds familiar."

"From inside the prison walls. Before you've arrived in the prison. The words are hidden from you."

"Is it night or day?"

"Both."

The rain burns.

I run for cover.

I try to pray.

The rain burns.

I run back to the sandwich man. "Does the rain burn you?" I ask.

The rain ceases.

He stops eating. He turns to me harshly. "Everything burns at the edge of obliteration," he says.

"Is that where we are? Is that a place?"

"Have you ever had ambrosia?" he asks, ignoring my questions.

"No."

"Neither have I. Just many large sandwiches."

"I'm hungry," I repeat.

"As am I," he says.

I run back to the beach. It's day now. I'm certain. "It's day!" I scream.

"It's *your lucky* day," a man says, zipping towards me ten feet off the ground. He has little wings near his feet.

"It acid rained on me. Or something. How is that lucky?"

"It's not. But you have a delivery. Three packages."

"And I haven't eaten anything in so long."

"I said *three packages*."

"Is one of them food?"

"Respect the commerce I bestow upon you and digitally sign for your packages." I sign his heart with my finger.

I sit in the sand. I hurriedly rip open the first box. It's small. Inside is a black placard with white letters that reads 'Freedom.'

The second package is much larger. I hope for an array of canned foods. Or an overstuffed sandwich.

I rip it open. I pull out bubble wrap and styrofoam and inflated plastic and cardboard. Inside is a 12x18 black frame with a black background and white letters that reads, 'Live. Laugh. Love.'

The third package disappears. Gone.

That one must've had food in it.

I saw the flying man in the distance. "More deliveries are to come," he shouts.

"Will there be food?"

"There will be more directions."

I force myself to laugh.

Ha ha

I search for a stick. I search for a rock. Hitting rock against end of stick again and again and again. *I will stab a fish and eat it.*

Again, and again, and again.

I tap the tip of the stick with my finger. Blood drips from the tip of my finger.

I stand to hunt my fish. But I can no longer see the ocean. I cannot. I cannot.

Arthur Tarley

notes for leaving

winter's never been   the place   for me
so I scratched its mortar

shed snowstorms and cannulas
from dry skin   unpicked

all that's been left to die
a card — *go love*

milk tooth   on the console
bleached with exits   hallway empty

as a tennis shoe   the quiet holds
threadbare friendships   to incant the air

and all those birthday lunches
mandated   endless Sundays   remember?

we'd wrap the leftovers   nobody wanted
to take home   in a map

outside the snowdrops' necks
hang   at the years

toes curl   the cold bones
of our childhood dog

beneath the apple tree's ghost
bury the keys

could you   this once
trust spring?

Antonia Taylor

A pride of lions

Safari Park

he observes
their closed habitat
a tin box
so small for six
how they squeal
as he pushes his nose
against the glass
regrets their lives
lived on the inside

Leo

purple hair and DMs
she cracks the hearts
of all the bull-shit boys
and how the girls
follow her trend
every flame she fires
even the sun
is her satellite

Coward

nothing could persuade
a cat with a yellow heart
to walk this road
without a song

Sea

his luminous body sits on the rock
a lighthouse on the headland
tempting her towards his circus

Dandelion

once he picked a flower
brought it to her door
she saw a stem without petals
he said
he was offering time
but it had blown away

Julia Usman

Birds

Black-capped chickadees grasp
the screen with their talons. Waiting for me

to fill their feeder. *They are the bravest*
birds my son says. *They almost never fly*

into the window and die. In shorts
on Black Friday I doomscroll

through bird books splashed with updated habitat maps.
The New York Times calls birds who don't have their own page

in the bird book *little trash birds.* A wail
of a scream in the night. Wings. In the morning

I show my son the rabbit. Curled in a bloodless
crescent moon. Only its head missing.

Lyndsey Kelly Weiner

About the Contributors

Moira Andrew has written poetry for children, and books on the creative arts for teachers. Her most recent collections of poetry are *Geese and Daughters*, (IDP), *Looking through Water,* (Poetry Space) and *Imagine a Kiss*, (D&W).

Lizzie Ballagher's work has appeared in magazines and webzines on either side of the Atlantic. Find her blog at https://lizzieballagherpoetry.wordpress.com/

Clare Bercot Zwerling is a newer poet. Her work appears in numerous journals and publications. She resides on the Mendocino Coast of California.

Margaret Beston is widely published, the author of two collections – *Long Reach River* (2014) and *Timepiece* (2019) – and also the founder of *Roundel* in Tonbridge.

Riley Burke is a student at George Washington University studying communications. She has poems published in *Polyphony Lit* (2018) and a self-published collection entitled *Aftershock*. She lives in Sacramento, California.

Sarah Butkovic recently received her Bachelor's Degree in English at Dominican University and aims to Master in Modern Literature. She is an aspiring writer, and plans on teaching or working in publishing upon graduation.

James Callan lives on the Kapiti Coast, New Zealand on a small farm with his wife, Rachel, and his little boy, Finn. His latest work is *Neon Dreams*, a science fiction novel.

Wendy Taylor Carlisle is the author of four books and five chapbooks and is the 2020 winner of the Phillip H. McMath Post-Publication Award for *The Mercy of Traffic.*

Richard Carpenter has been writing poetry since retiring. He is a member of York Stanza. He has a self-published collection of poems concerning the adventures of Dippy after leaving The Natural History Museum: *Dippy Thumbs a Lift*.

Joseph Chaplain is a new writer currently living in the Peak District. His short fiction has been published by Crystal Peake in their *Dark Folklore* anthology.

Allison Collins is a journalist and editor, with fiction published by Blast Furnace Press, Havok, Shark Reef, and Easy Street. Allison lives in upstate New York with her family.

Nigel Ferrier Collins is a writer and visual artist whose poems have appeared in magazines including *Poetry Review*. In a career in education he contributed to journals and had books published by OUP and Heinemann.

Annemarie Cooper lives in Tower Hamlets and has had poems in various magazines. She has two published pamphlets: *Seeds* (Flarestack) and *The Flight of Birds* (Soaring Penguin). She loves walking and gardening.

Charlotte Cosgrove is a poet and teacher from Liverpool. She is published in *Dreich, Trouvaille Review* and *The Literary Yard*. She has work forthcoming in *Beyond Words* and *Confingo*.

Erin K. Davis is a multimedia artist and writer with a degree in Creative Writing from the University of Houston. Her most recent collections of poetry include *Ribbon of Darkness Over Me, Aridity*, and *A Girlhood in Fragments*.

Sara Davis is a member of Roundel poets in Kent. Her poems have been published in *South Poetry* and in the collection *Links in the Chain*. She is joint winner of the Sir Philip Sydney poetry prize 2020.

R C de Winter writes in several genres with a focus on poetry, which appears in several top literary journals. Her work is also included in many anthologies.

A poet, educator, and artist, Andrea Janelle Dickens' work has recently appeared in *New South, Ruminate*, and *The Wayfarer*, among others.

Brian Docherty is the Beach Bard of St. Leonards. He has published eight books, most recently *The View From the Villa Delirium*, (Dempsey & Windle, 2021).

William Dubie teaches at the University of Massachusetts Lowell. His poems have appeared in many literary, small press, and college publications.

Willow J Fields's (@willows_field) recent titles include, *Casualty of History* (flash fiction), *A Break-In Reality* (short story) and *The Humidified Series* (flash fiction).

Jim Friedman lives in Beeston, Nottinghamshire. On retirement he took up writing poetry again. He is a member of the Derby Stanza group.

Timothy Kenny's fiction and nonfiction has appeared in more than two dozen U.S. and European magazines. His essay collection *Far Country, Stories From Abroad and Other Places*, was published in 2015 and nominated for a Pushcart Prize.

A novelist and poet, Ian Gouge is the creator of **Coverstory** *books* and the driving force behind *New Contexts*. His latest works include *On Parliament Hill* (a novel) and *The Homelessness of a Child* (poetry).

Gill Learner's poetry has been widely published and won several awards, including the Hamish Canham Prize 2008. Her third collection, *Change* (Two Rivers Press) is due in October 2021.

Michael Lund is author of *At Home and Away*, a novel series that chronicles an American family from 1915 to 2015, and two volumes of short stories related to military experience.

Jayden Martin is a First Nations poet and writer with disability from Australia. His works have appeared in anthologies by *The Poet's Haven* and *Wingless Dreamer*.

Penny McCarthy, commended in Poetry Business and Poetry London competitions, has published one pamphlet, *The Stealing Shadow*, and poems in *Ambit, LRB, Stand*.

Alfie Ormsbee (he/him) is a transgender poet and English teacher from Michigan. His latest work will be featured in *The Heart of Pride* anthology by Quillkeepers Press.

Carol Park loves exploring Asia and her native California. Find her poetry online at MiGoZine and Monterey Review. Her fiction at CarolPark.us. Her novel set is forthcoming.

Janet Philo is published online and in print. Her two pamphlets include: *Cheap Fish for Kings* (Black Light Engine Room, 2020). She also has work included in *The Best New British and Irish Poets 2019-2021* (The Black Spring Press Group)

Jenna Plewes's latest collections *A Woven Rope* (V.Press) and *The Salt and Sweet of Memory* (Dempsey and Windle) are both being sold by her in aid of Freedom from Torture. Find her on Poetry PF or on Facebook.

David Punter lives and works in Bristol, and has published eight poetry collections, the latest of which are *Those Other Fields* (Palewell, 2020) and *Stranger* (Cinnamon, 2021).

Jenny Robb has written poetry since retiring. In 2020/21 she's been published in online and print magazines, and anthologies. Her debut pamphlet will be published by Yaffle in 2021.

Gillie Robic was born in India and lives in London. Her collections, *Swimming Through Marble* and *Lightfalls*, were published by Live Canon in 2016 and 2019.

Stephen Roe is a retired Lancashire Secondary Headteacher living in Accrington and for several months of each year in France. He is a Poetry Society member of the Ribble Valley Stanza group.

Graeme Ryan was born in Lancashire and now lives near Exmoor. A Drama teacher and playwright for many years, he has now returned to poetry, his work featuring on *Bard Window* and in a range of competitions and publications.

Yvonne Sampson has had stories and plays shortlisted for many competitions, including the BBC Writersroom Prize. She recently won second prize in the Green Stories competition.

Barbara Sapienza, a retired clinical psychologist and novelist - *Anchor Out*, 2017; *The Laundress*, 2020 - lives with her husband in Sausalito and is working on a memoir.

Recently "retired" from working in local government and the voluntary sector, Helen Scadding is now focusing on writing and volunteering. Her poetry has recently been published in *Artemis*, *South* and *Reach Poetry*.

Dave Smith, a retired English teacher, is certain that the perceptive fellow-poets in Derby Stanza have been vital in helping him to find his voice.

David Smith lives and writes in North Yorkshire where he conducts Creative Writing classes. His work has appeared in *The Sid Chaplin Short Story Anthology*, *Red Squirrel Press* and *Assent*. His third collection is *The Stencil Room* (2018).

Kathleen Strafford s the author of two collections of poetry: *Her Own Language & Wilderness of Skin*. She is chief editor of Runcible Spoon webzine & publishing.

Kate Swann is a Northern, rural poet with an eye for detail. Family, friends and travel are important to her life and none escape her pen when she is writing.

Arthur Tarley is a writer, activist, and union member. His work has appeared in *Current Affairs* and *The Dillydoun Review*, and his as yet unpublished novel is *Built Upon Freedom*.

Antonia Taylor is a British Cypriot writer, poet and communications expert. She lives in Reading and is currently working on her first collection.

Julia Usman has had numerous articles and poems published in the UK and Australia. Her debut collection *She Who Sings Is Not Always Happy* was published by Coverstory Books (2021). She lives in Swaledale, North Yorkshire.

Lyndsey Kelly Weiner is a graduate of Stonecoast MFA and teaches writing at Syracuse University. She blogs at haikuveg.com.

Recent publications from **Coverstory** *books*

New Contexts: 1

Globally the number of people being creative with language is truly extraordinary. While each of us will have our individual reasons for writing, many of them common, where the majority come together is in the desire to be read.

There are lots of outlets for writers, contributing to an ever-expanding and increasingly densely populated literary landscape, and people continue to submit to competitions, journals and magazines. In the vast majority of cases we do so not for financial reward but for recognition, to be validated, to have a 'readership'.

When it comes to publication, of the two deciding factors - talent and luck - the latter is the most fickle.

The idea for *New Contexts* was born from all of the above. The goal, to harvest a small sample of good unpublished writing and create an anthology to showcase it.

Joyriding Down Utopia Avenue by Simon French

"Readers of Simon French's debut collection *Joyriding Down Utopia Avenue* are in a for a delightfully jolt-filled, dodgem-car ride. People search for thrills, only to find them deflating into disillusionment. Yet elsewhere there are tender, moving and funny encounters in suburbia. Turns and twists of perspective abound, surprising, often shocking and sometimes mystifying us. What we thought we had experienced shifts dramatically, and we need to re-think what we have witnessed.

"The ride may be occasionally bumpy but French has a firm grasp of his wheel. His forms are spare, pared down, and his sensuous descriptive skills and playful wit excite the ear. He has a beady eye for focussing on details that make his places and subjects become vividly present. Happiness may be rare, hard-won, but the verbal fun and psychological thoughtfulness on offer means that riding with French down Utopia Avenue is never dull and more than joyful." - Jim Friedman

She Who Sings Is Not Always Happy by Julia Usman

"Julia Usman's poetry invites us into her childhood landscape of farm and meadows, schooldays, and travels in France, Brussels, Milan and beyond. It is poetry at ease in all those environments. Her close observations and reflections are delicately woven into 'Finding a voice', 'Still Life' and many more. This is a collection deeply layered with longing and grace for people loved and times gone, poetry I want to read again and again. Beautiful." - Kerry Darbishire

"Julia Usman's poetry ranges from inner landscape to outer; through memories of her own childhood, growing up on a farm in her beloved Yorkshire, woven through with memories of others. They are deeply rooted in place, yet her sensitive observations of people and place also travel. The poems sing of joy and loss; of pain and beauty. Her poems are spare and clear, they remind me of spring water, yet they allow breathing space for the reader to enter. Whether read individually, or as a whole, this collection is of its time, yet timeless. A collection to savour." - Geraldine Green

On Parliament Hill by Ian Gouge

Her voice is a trigger; a voice which forces Neil to relive the crises and failures of his past, and which offers him the possibility of a positive new future. But before he can decide on what he wants the life ahead of him to look like - and her role in it - he must pass judgement on himself.

Ian Gouge's novels focus on individuals who are trying to come to terms with their histories; characters facing a struggle, legacies from which they have to find a way to free themselves.

The Homelessness of a Child by Ian Gouge

By the time Ian Gouge went to university he had already lived in seventeen different places - houses, pre-fabs, flats, rooms of one sort or another - and all within the environs of the same two towns on the south coast of England. No single location more than four miles from the next, between some you could have measured the distance in hundreds of yards.

A number of these accommodations had been emergency refuges provided by the Local Authority to stave off homelessness, but in reality, every single residence proved temporary. Exactly at a time when a child needed security, the very notions of 'home', 'family' - even 'love' - were being challenged, their meanings redefined, shaken to their core; experiences which scarred both an upbringing and the future which followed it.

In the major thread of *The Homelessness of a Child*, the poet reflects on that childhood, explores its events and repercussions. Inevitably it is both a passionate and dispassionate retelling, the latter a result of the detachment a young boy would learn to adopt in order to protect himself from the chaos of the world he was forced to inhabit.

Pins & Feathers by Kate Miller, Emma Blowers, and Erin Thompson

Coverstory books is thrilled to be bringing to market its first collection of plays. These three plays, all produced by Hertfordshire-based community theatre 'Pins & Feathers', tell extraordinary stories of ordinary people. With emotion and humour, they bring history to life, portraying characters challenged by events beyond their control, whose defiant voices resonate today.

- **The Last Witch**, by Kate Miller
- **Seeing it Through**, by Kate Miller, Emma Blowers and Erin Thompson
- **The March**, by Kate Miller

Stepping Westward by Berta Lawrence

The hill country of West Somerset is famous for its association with the Romantic poets, Coleridge and Wordsworth, whose *Lyrical Ballads* (1798) emerged out of their experience of the area and revolutionised English poetry. It was 130 years later that a young teacher, Berta Lawrence, came to live in the same part of the county.

Over the next seventy years, inspired by its landscape and legends, she wrote a succession of books and novels. She also wrote poems, over fifty of which were published in a local journal. After her death, more than two hundred poems were discovered among her papers, some published, some in typescript, and some in hand-written drafts. Here for the first time *Stepping Westward* gathers up the best of these, critically edited by Tom Furniss. They show how the storied Somerset landscape and the natural cycle of its rural year continue to inspire and delight.

Lightning Source UK Ltd.
Milton Keynes UK
UKHW010107060921
390023UK00001B/7